SOUTHEAST ASIA

A NEW YORK TIMES BYLINE BOOK

SOUTHEAST ASIA by TILLMAN DURDIN
AFRICA by WALDEMAR A. NIELSEN
RUSSIA by HARRISON E. SALISBURY
CHINA by HARRY SCHWARTZ
LATIN AMERICA by TAD SZULC
THE MIDDLE EAST by JAY WALZ

NEW YORK TIMES BYLINE BOOKS

SOUTHEAST ASIA

by Tillman Durdin

A NEW YORK TIMES BYLINE BOOK

ATHENEUM

NEW YORK

1966

CONTENTS

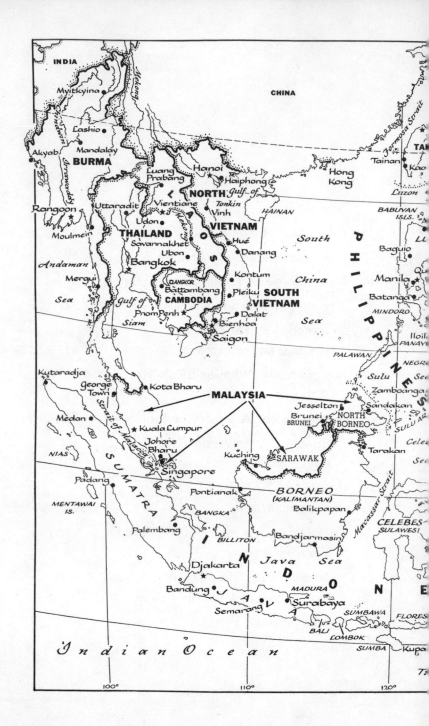

0 MILES 500

TROPIC OF CANCER

20°

Pacific

MARIANAS

SAIPAN
TINIAN

GUAM

Ocean

10°

TRUK

DANAO

PALAU

CAROLINE ISLANDS

HALMAHERA

EQUATOR

0°

BIAK

Sorong

Kotabaru
(Hollandia)

NEW
IRELAND

Wewak

Rabaul

CERAM

NEW BRITAIN

Amboina

Kaimana

WEST IRIAN

Mt.Carstenz

Juliana Top

NORTH-EAST
NEW GUINEA

Lae

Finschafen

NEW

Mt.Hagen

Salamaua

ARU
IS.

PAPUA

Buna

GUINEA

Port
Moresby

10°

Arafura

Sea

Coral

Torres Strait

140°

Sea

150°

Darwin
130°

AUSTRALIA

C. E. MC DONNELL – D. BROWNSTEIN N. Y. TIMES MAP DEPT.

SOUTHEAST ASIA

A NEW YORK TIMES BYLINE BOOK

I

Crossroads of Contending Forces

THE MUFFLED THUD of explosions jarred us awake two hours before dawn on December 8, 1941. My wife and I jumped from our bed at the Adelphi Hotel in Singapore and threw ourselves on the floor as the blasts grew louder and nearer. We knew what was happening. For days the British High Command had been reporting big new concentrations of Japanese warships and planes in southern Indochina, 500 miles to the north, and we had been expecting an attack. The explosions meant the Japanese offensive in Southeast Asia had begun with an air raid on the great port and military base of Singapore.

The bombs destroyed many houses and killed many people, but missed the venerable Adelphi.

Minutes after the air raid ended we were up, dressed, and running through the streets to press headquarters a few blocks away. There we learned that the Japanese were landing troops in Thailand and also in northern Malaya, where the British were fighting for control of the beaches and air-fields.

As a war correspondent for *The New York Times* I sent an urgent dispatch reporting that the big push was on. It was a bigger push than I knew at the time. Later the news came in that the Japanese had also bombed Pearl Harbor in Hawaii and had attacked the Philippines. It was clear that the Japanese had set out to conquer all Southeast Asia and, by striking at Hawaii, hoped to prevent United States forces from coming to the aid of the area's defenders.

Temporarily, the Japanese succeeded. Within six months they had overrun every part of Southeast Asia—Burma, Thailand, Malaya, Singapore, British Borneo, the Dutch East Indies and the Philippines—in addition to the Indochinese region they had occupied earlier. But their triumph was short-lived. Recovering from the destruction at Pearl Harbor, the United States thrust across the Pacific and with its British, French, and Dutch allies drove the Japanese all the way back to Japan in four years of terrible fighting. The battles and devastation of World War II were the worst the Southeast Asians had ever experienced.

The Japanese invaded and the Allies retook Southeast Asia because it is a world crossroads and one of the richest and most desirable regions on earth. Stretching southward from the great land mass of China and eastward from the Indian subcontinent, it lies across the sea routes between China and India and between East and West. Its location and its fertile lands, natural seaports, mineral wealth and soft tropical climate have made it the goal of migrating hordes and conquerors since the dawn of history. Always a weak conglomeration of separate states and diverse peoples, Southeast Asia has never had the strength to resist invasions from outside or the unity to avoid conflict in its own communities.

Thus the Japanese invasion repeated a familiar pattern, but it hastened the birth of a new era. The Japanese drove out the Western powers that had established themselves as colonial rulers during the two centuries before 1941. These powers—Britain, France, the Netherlands and the United States—in turn ousted the Japanese, but when they resumed their old positions they discovered they could no longer remain there.

Even before the Japanese occupation the Southeast Asians had begun to struggle for an end to Western colonial rule. Japan's early wartime victories showed them that the Western colonial powers could be conquered. The Southeast Asians, who were brutally mistreated by the Japanese, became extremely intense in their desire for independence. When the colonial powers returned, liberation movements grew throughout the area. The United States quickly fulfilled a prewar pledge and gave the Philippines its freedom. The other powers—the British in Burma, Malaya, Singapore and Borneo; the French in Indochina (now South Vietnam, North Vietnam, Cambodia and Laos); and the Dutch in the East Indies (now Indonesia)—moved more slowly, but eventually they too yielded to the demand for independence, either voluntarily or as a result of rebellions against them.

Independence, however, has not put an end to outside aggression or internal strife in Southeast Asia. Supported by Communist China and to a lesser degree by the Soviet Union, Communists in South Vietnam and Laos today are fighting to take over those two Indochinese countries. In addition, Indonesia is making sporadic guerrilla attacks on the new nation of Malaysia. Formed in 1963 from the former British colonies of Malaya, Singapore, Sarawak and Sabah, Malaysia now exists without Singapore, following this territory's withdrawal from the union in 1965. In Burma ethnic minorities and Communist factions periodically fight the government.

The continuing turmoil has had repercussions around the globe. British, Australian and New Zea-

land troops have been helping to combat the Indonesian guerrillas in Malaysia, and the United States
is deeply committed in South Vietnam to a war
against the Communist Vietcong and their North
Vietnamese sponsors. By late 1965 roughly 150,-
000 American troops were engaged in bitter conflict
in South Vietnam; U.S. planes were daily pounding
Vietcong positions in South Vietnam and raiding
military objectives in North Vietnam. American
casualty lists continued to grow, and contingents of
Australian and New Zealand troops had also joined
the Vietnam struggle. More than ever, Southeast
Asia had become the focus of controversy and attention, the possible cockpit of a new world war.

Mounting American concern with United States
military intervention in Vietnam erupted in 1965
into street demonstrations, sit-ins and passionate de-
bates. At a series of teach-ins on scores of college
campuses across the country, professors and students excitedly opposed or supported Washington's
actions in Vietnam. On May 5, 1965, at Washington's Sheraton-Park Hotel ballroom, professors
from many universities gathered with government
officials to criticize and defend Washington's policies in Vietnam while the nation watched on television.

Dr. Hans J. Morgenthau of the University of Chi-
cago, one of the critics, said in effect that the United
States was hopelessly bogged down in a war in

South Vietnam that the South Vietnamese people did not support and the United States could not win. He declared that the United States should seek an agreement that would end the fighting, let the Vietnamese of the Communist North and the anti-Communist South vote to reunite the country, and permit the United States to withdraw. He argued that Southeast Asia was properly in the Chinese sphere of influence and that the United States could not change this and should not try to do so.

Dr. Morgenthau was opposed by Professor Robert A. Scalapino of the University of California and by others who maintained that the South Vietnamese did not want to be ruled by Communist tyranny and that Washington had an obligation to help them. They argued that the United States could win the Vietnamese war and should do so to prevent all Southeast Asia from becoming Communist and a sphere of Chinese domination. The Americans who are fighting in Vietnam are puzzled and dismayed by the Americans back home who criticize what the United States is doing in Vietnam.

The pro-Communist Southeast Asians, of course, denounce us while the anti-Communists applaud us. Nai Thanat Khoman, the Foreign Minister of Thailand, said, "We don't want to join the slave camp. That is why each and every one of the 31 million people of Thailand supports the policy of the United States."

The United States government has tried to help Southeast Asia's newly independent nations remain free, not only by sending Americans to fight in Vietnam but also by providing military, economic and other aid to the region. In the Philippines, Thailand and Malaysia hundreds of members of the Peace Corps are working to improve schools, grow better crops, build roads and cure the sick as part of United States assistance programs in Southeast Asia. We have spent billions of dollars to construct dams and highways, equip hospitals and factories, expand education and train and arm defense forces.

As American troops try to help halt Communist aggression, we risk getting involved in a big war, perhaps with Communist China. Plainly, Southeast Asia is for Americans not just a remote tropical region with romantic names like Singapore, Bali and Bangkok but a part of the world that is intimately linked with our own destiny.

II

From Ancient Days to
Modern Ways

SOUTHEAST ASIA extends more than 3,000 miles from east to west, more than 2,000 miles from north to south. With less than half the actual land mass of the United States, its population of approximately 245 million outnumbers that of the United States by about 50 million.

Southeast Asia forms a vast fragmented horseshoe around the South China Sea. On the west it sprawls from the northern tip of Burma in the Himalayas down through Laos, Vietnam, Cambodia, Thailand and the Malaysian state of Malaya to Singapore. The Indonesian islands, some 3,000 altogether, roughly form the southern rim of the horseshoe. The eastern segment is made up of Borneo, where Malaysian Sarawak and Sabah border

Indonesian Kalimantan, and the 7,000 islands of the Philippines.

Southeast Asia is an immense mass of rugged and trackless mountains cloaked with forests; rice-growing river deltas and coastal plains; fertile inland plateaus; endless stretches of tangled, often swampy jungle; and many, many islands. The patterns of the mountains and rivers, as well as the scattered islands, have created barriers not only between countries but also between communites.

Two of the world's mightiest rivers, the Mekong and the Salween, with headwaters in the mountains of Tibet, flow through deep gorges in the northern reaches of Southeast Asia and end in soggy deltas. These and other shorter rivers, such as the Irrawaddy in Burma, the Chao Phraya in Thailand, the Red River in North Vietnam and the Tonle Sap in Cambodia, play a vital part in the economic life of their areas. In the monsoon belt, wet and dry seasons alternate; outside it the lowlands are hot and humid the year round. Altitude brings coolness and the 18,000-foot mountain peaks in northern Burma, the highest in Southeast Asia, are snow-covered.

This diverse, often spectacularly beautiful natural setting is the backdrop for a fascinating mixture of the primitive and the modern. Cities of more than a million people—such as Bangkok, Manila, Singapore and Jakarta—with Western-styled high-rise buildings and automobile-clogged streets spread into rice-growing countrysides where peasants still plow with water buffaloes and live in little wooden houses built on stilts. Jet airliners take off from big municipal airports and in a few minutes are flying over mountains inhabited by tribesmen who wear almost no clothes and still hunt with poisoned darts.

At Luang Prabang, King Savang Vatthana of Laos lives in a French-style palace with Western decor, but for official ceremonies he dons the baggy *panung,* the pantaloons worn by his ancestors for a thousand years.

On the Indonesian island of Bali, barefoot men and girls perform their elegant traditional dances in dusty village squares and then go to see a John Wayne movie at the local theater. Textile mills and automobile assembly plants operate on the outskirts of bustling urban centers not far from where villagers stand in mud and water to transplant green rice shoots by hand just as their ancestors have done for centuries.

Of Southeast Asia the anthropologist Cora Du Bois has said, "There is probably no other area of the world so richly endowed with diverse cultural strains." Yet there is a similarity in the physical appearance of most Southeast Asians. Except for the Vietnamese, who are yellow, resemble Chinese and in fact migrated originally from the coastal provinces of China, the majority of people in all Southeast Asian countries are round-eyed, black-haired, short, slight and brown-skinned—some darker and some lighter than others. They are the descendants of Malay-Indonesian stock who came 1,500 to 2,500 years ago from the interior of Asia and mixed with the small, dark-skinned earlier inhabitants of Southeast Asia. Some of them still survive in the uplands. Among these are the little Negritos of Malaya and the Philippines and certain mountain tribesmen of Vietnam and Laos who shift their primitive gardens from one jungle clearing to another as they grow opium that eventually is smuggled out as heroin and morphine to countries all over the world.

The brown-skinned lowland majority of Southeast Asians settled into their valleys and plains as fishermen, rice growers and craftsmen. About the time of Christ they began to be influenced by the higher cultures of China and India through contacts with traders, explorers, priests, teachers and military invaders. The new influences blended with the native cultures and, combined with the Western features of more recent times, produced the colorful crossroads culture found today.

The Indians at first brought Hinduism and Buddhism and the characteristic folklore, crafts and architecture of these faiths. Later they implanted Islam. The Chinese came with their Confucian philosophy, their Buddhist-Taoist religious concepts, their silk, porcelain and other trade goods. They conquered and then ruled the people of Vietnam for a thousand years until 939 A.D., making these tough, wiry Southeast Asians culturally Chinese.

Neither the Indians nor the Chinese made conquests elsewhere in Southeast Asia, but they did spread their arts, myths and ideas. In addition, the Indian influence produced leaders and religious practices of powerful significance. Southeast Asian chiefs found in the Hindu-Buddhist rites a way to establish supernatural sanction for their rule. They became, in effect, god-kings as in the great Khmer Empire, which from the 9th to the 15th century extended over most of present-day Cambodia, Thailand, South Vietnam and Laos, and also in the Indonesian empires of Shrivijaya and Madjapahit during roughly the same period. Buddhism from Ceylon eventually triumphed almost everywhere over Hinduism at about the same time.

Islam spread through the Indonesian islands, and Christianity was introduced by the first Spanish and Portuguese to the Philippines and the Moluccas of eastern Indonesia. No old faiths or customs were entirely displaced; the new was simply accepted and added to the old. By the 17th century the many influences that had been brought to bear on Southeast Asia had forged patterns that persist to this day. Burma, Thailand, Cambodia and Laos had become Buddhist and culturally and politically similar. The Vietnamese had adopted the culture and institutions of China. Most of the people of the Malay Peninsula and Indonesia had accepted Islam, although Christianity had begun to take root through Portuguese and Dutch influence; the little Indonesian island of Bali remained staunchly Hindu—thousands of miles removed from the nearest Hindu community in India. The Philippines was still largely tribal, but Spanish conquerors had begun the process of turning the islands into Southeast Asia's first and only Christian nation.

The colonization begun by the Spanish in the Philippines and the Portuguese and Dutch in the East Indies eventually added a cover of modern Western culture to all the preceding layers of religion, customs and art.

The colonizers were lured by trade, particularly in the spices of the East Indies, and by adventure and the desire to increase the power of their respective countries.

The Portuguese came first, capturing Malacca on the west coast of the Malay Peninsula in 1511 and expanding from this base into the Moluccas of the East Indies to get a monopoly on the cloves, nutmeg and other spices that grew there. A century later the Dutch drove the Portuguese out and made the East Indies a Dutch colony. The Spanish took over the Philippines.

By the late 19th century the British had established themselves as the colonial power in Burma, the Malay Peninsula (Malaya), Singapore and the

Borneo territories of Sarawak, North Borneo (now Sabah) and Brunei. The French had taken over the Indochinese kingdoms of Vietnam, Cambodia and Laos.

By shrewdly playing the colonial powers off against each other, accepting Western influences and avoiding provocations Siam (now Thailand) managed to escape conquest; today it is the only Southeast Asian country that was never colonialized. Through its defeat of Spain in the Spanish-American War the United States took possession of the Philippines, coming late on the scene as a Southeast Asian colonial power. The Portuguese managed to retain one tiny foothold, the eastern half of the little island of Timor, just north of Australia. In one of the small ironies of history, all the other Western powers have given up their colonies in Southeast Asia; but Portugal, which came first, remains longest, sharing Timor today with Indonesia.

In the span of Southeast Asia's history the Western colonial era was comparatively brief, but it made a deep mark. It brought not only such things as railways, airlines, modern roads, modern ports and modern means of communication but also new political, social, esthetic and religious concepts. Now independent, the countries of Southeast Asia are struggling to reconcile this heritage of colonialism with their own traditional pre-Western patterns.

The outcome of the struggle will determine

whether the nations of Southeast Asia can retain control of their destinies in a combination of the old and the new or whether they will come once again under outside domination. There is a danger of such domination in the international rivalries touched off by the Communist drive for power in the area.

The stakes are high. Except for Indonesia with its population of 105 million, its large military forces and its expansionist policies, the countries of Southeast Asia represent no threat outside the region. But if they were under the domination of powerful outside forces, they could constitute a threat.

Southeast Asia is a vital transit zone for round-the-world shipping and air transportation. Its resources, moreover, are a prize of great value. Southeast Asia is the world's largest exporter of natural rubber, copra, quinine, kapok, rice, teak, pepper, tapioca flour and tin. It produces significant quantities of sugar, tea, coffee, tobacco, sisal, tropical fruits, essential oils, spices, natural resins and gums, petroleum and large amounts of iron ore and bauxite.

For all these reasons the future of this fascinating and diverse area is beyond any doubt a matter of global concern.

III

Kaleidoscope of Lands and Peoples

In THIS AGE of air transportation and mass tourism, travelers usually approach Southeast Asia through one of its big semi-Westernized cities like Manila, Singapore or Bangkok. There the feel and color of the area are almost swallowed up by the tall modern buildings, the automobiles, the shop windows bulging with the world's latest products, and the pedestrians often dressed like their counterparts in New York, Paris, St. Louis or Buenos Aires.

I like much better the way I first encountered Southeast Asia—not through a great capital or coastal metropolis, but through a "back door" that opened abruptly and dramatically onto the region's tropical landscape and human pageantry.

In the summer of 1941, before Pearl Harbor but

in the fourth year of the Chinese-Japanese war, I
flew from the wartime Chinese capital, Chungking,
to the Chinese city of Kunming on the first lap of a
trip. From Kunming I drove southward with a cou-
ple of Chinese and another American along the rugged, winding Burma Road. Scurrying off the road
occasionally to hide from raiding Japanese planes,
we traveled toward the Burmese frontier for three
days through the grim, rocky, barren mountains of
China's Yunnan Province.

Then suddenly, as we rounded a bend, we saw
ahead and below a beautiful green valley dotted
with clumps of palm and bamboo trees and tiny villages of thatch-covered houses on stilts. Soon we began to pass stalls of luscious-looking mangoes, ba-
nanas, papayas and coconuts and we stopped to buy
some from the smiling Shan people who lived in the
valley. The air was gentle and warm, the whole
countryside lush with the green profusion of the
tropics, and everywhere there was evidence of a soft,
easygoing life. It all contrasted sharply with the bare
mountains, the stone- and tile-roofed houses and the
harsh Chinese existence we had left behind us. This
valley, we realized, was where Southeast Asia began.

We crossed the border and spent the night in a
crowded little hotel in Lashio, the crossroads of
northern Burma. There we saw the varied peoples
of the Burma-China border area: cheerful Shans,
the men in baggy white trousers and towel-like tur-

bans, the women in close-fitting, long black skirts; wiry little Kachin men, the fighters of the region, in khaki shorts and open shirts; Burmese men and women in peacock-colored skirtlike *longyis* knotted in the front. They thronged dusty streets lined with ramshackle wooden shops that were run, as is customary in Southeast Asia, by Chinese and Indians.

These shops sold simple factory-made or hand-crafted household items and brightly colored cloth from China, India and the West. Street stalls and small restaurants served succulent Chinese dishes or hot Indian and Burmese curries. An open-air market, noisy with bargaining buyers, was piled high with golden fruits, trinkets, wicker baskets, vegetables, melons, tea leaves, handwoven Shan carry-all shoulder bags and gnarled roots for use as charms or medicines. Up one alleyway a withered old hill woman squatted before her display of pots and pans and bamboo combs, chewing betel nuts which brilliantly redden the mouth and blacken the teeth. Three-wheeled pedicabs, bicycles, oxcarts and an occasional car or jeep maneuvered through the crowds of people. Pedicabs are two-seater rickshaws with modified tricycle wheels or a motorcycle engine.

It was a tropical, cheerful, motley scene typical not of China, India or Japan but of Southeast Asia. With some variations in the physical characteristics and colorful costumes of the people and in the native architecture, I have seen it in every Southeast Asian country.

There are two striking but complementary aspects of living in Southeast Asia. One is the delightful diversity of people, language and custom. The other is that, in spite of this mosaic of differences, there is everywhere a basic similarity in environment, tempo and ways of life.

In 1958 I spent a month in the little city of Padang, which faces the Indian Ocean on the west coast of Sumatra, Indonesia's big oil-producing island. To relax occasionally from my job reporting on a rebellion there against the Indonesian government, I used to go to a long, curving beach five miles from Padang to swim and lie briefly under the hot sun.

Coconut palms mingled with clumps of mangrove trees that grew at the water's edge. Fishing nets were stretched out to dry. A few tiny, hand-built fishing boats were tied up to palm tree trunks. Offshore was the silhouette of a miniature jungle-covered island. Monkeys broke a warm and lazy silence with their chatter. Far down the beach a little thatch-covered bamboo shack on stilts marked a fisherman's home. This, I thought as I lay on the shining sand, was the typical Southeast Asian landscape, from Burma's shores on the Bay of Bengal down and across to the coasts of Halmahera in eastern Indonesia.

But one cannot reduce Southeast Asia to this single panorama, common as it is. Other scenes are just as typical: rice fields, for example, shimmering with water, reflecting white clouds floating across wide plains to distant blue mountains; rice terraces climbing in green geometry to the summits of hills; little canals and rivers busy with an endless traffic of junks, sampans and houseboats; and vast stretches of rain-swept, leech-infested jungle inhabited by tigers, birds, monkeys and sometimes by a few primitive natives hiding from the outside world—the kind of jungle that for centuries completely hid the Khmer Empire's massive temples and palaces from the Cambodian peasants living their whole lives only a few miles away.

Over all Southeast Asia, except for high plateaus and mountaintops, the weather is hot; heavy monsoon rains simply make the hot air more humid. Throughout the area the people are generally more easygoing than the Chinese and gayer than the Indians. Westerners generally find them pleasant, gentle and tolerant, although the history of the region shows they also have a formidable capacity for cruelty and violence.

In all Southeast Asia except Vietnam, which bears many marks of a thousand years of Chinese cultural influence, the traditional house is built up on poles, off the frequently monsoon-flooded or snake-infested ground. Everywhere the green, golden or flooded rice fields stretch out from crowded little villages, showing a basic peasant economy. Everywhere the massive, plodding water buffalo is the most important work animal. Almost everywhere the staple diet is fish, rice and fruits that grow virtually without care. Often food is cooked once a day—in the morning—and is available cold at any time for the family and visiting friends and relatives.

In Southeast Asia there is a natural flair for color, for gay scarfs or bags or clothing. Everywhere are seen the same sorts of little objects for household or personal use, woven or carved through the centuries by rough but deft peasant hands. People of traditional habits chew the teeth-blackening betel nut, drink a mildly alcoholic fermented palm juice and like to eat a big round fruit called a durian which smells like a rotten egg to the newcomer.

Long ago, because of incessant wars, the peoples of Southeast Asia doubtless knew something about their neighbors. But when their countries became Western colonies these people had little contact with one another and grew very ignorant about nearby lands. Since they gained independence and began to develop some relations with each other, they have become intrigued by previously unknown similarities. When Cambodians saw the ruins of the huge Buddhist temple at Borobudur, Java, and the nearby Hindu temples of Prembanen on Java, they compared these with their own magnificent Hindu-

Buddhist ruins of Angkor and saw before them, in carved stone, evidence that Moslem Indonesia had once, like themselves, experienced a great Buddhist-Hindu period under Indian influence. The Malayans and the Indonesians were delighted to discover that the Tagalog language spoken in the Philippines had such a common ancestry with their own tongue that they could sometimes catch the drift of Tagalog conversation. The Balinese, Cambodians, Laotians, Thais and Burmese have found a basic similarity in the delicate hand and body gestures of their beautiful formal dances, all deriving from an ancient cultural debt to India.

In contrast to the pattern of similarities in Southeast Asia is the charm of its infinite variety. Every land, every people, has its own distinctive qualities —a special festival or religious rite, a special sauce or flavor, a special taboo or form of courtesy, a special type of amusement or drama.

Only in Bali, for instance, is artistic creativity so integral a part of daily life, so alive in music, dance, temple carvings, festival processions, harvest fetes and hand-made objects for the gods or the home. Only in Laos do young men and young women engage in a charming ritualistic group duet combining wit and lovemaking. It is Indonesia's Minangkebau community that produces Southeast Asia's matriarchal society; when a man marries, he goes to live under the thick upswept roofs of the traditional house of his wife's family and is subject to the domination of his mother-in-law. It is the Thais who courteously construct, in front of their homes, tiny dwellings for the spirits and place there pleasing offerings.

Of all the peoples making betel-nut boxes, it is the Cambodians who so artfully designed intricate silver reproductions of spirits and animals. Only the Thais have built temples and palaces with distinctive *three*-tiered slanted roofs of glittering gold and green tile, ending at the corners with an inexpressibly airy up-sweep of serpents' tails. Only in Burma do men universally persist in their traditional dress, splashing city and countryside with color in their crisp turbans and gay *longyis*.

Many Southeast Asian women wear some version or adaptation of the skirtlike sarong, but there is a world of difference between the Japanese lady's intricately patterned, brown and beige batik-designed sarong and the Laotian's brilliantly colored skirt threaded with silver and gold. Filipino women, with a soft fullness, just a hint of the voluptuousness their sisters in Southeast Asia lack, are beautiful in huge butterfly sleeves as they dance with men wearing blue tunic-shirts of embroidered organdy.

The slender Vietnamese, her long black hair pulled straight back from her lovely oval face, wears perhaps the most attractive traditional costume. In spite of years of war and terrorism—the bomb exploding suddenly in a crowded street—graceful Vietnamese girls still stroll down the French-built boulevards of Saigon in their loose white silk trousers covered—or, more accurately, revealed—by a white or colored silk robe slit up each side to meet, at a tiny waist, a long-sleeved, high-collared tight-fitting bodice.

Aside from exotic traditional garb, nothing contributes more to the colorful variety of Southeast Asia than the old and the new standing side by side —modern machines and primitive practices, the 10th century and the 20th century—jostling each other.

Many Filipinos who fly in planes, watch television, have university degrees and manage up-to-date businesses still consult "witch doctors" who practice magic. One Filipino friend of mine says he knew in advance, from someone who could see into the future, that President Ramon Magsaysay was going to be killed in the air crash that took his life in March, 1957.

President Sukarno of Indonesia, a Moslem who collects new titles, beautiful women and modern art, is said to pray to his *kris,* the dagger sacred to Malayans through the centuries. He also collaborates with 20th-century Communism while seeking omens and prophecies of the kind that guided princes in the courts of Java a thousand years ago. In fact, it might be said that one of the biggest factors in the Indonesian leader's misgovernment is his inability to integrate the old and the new.

In Southeast Asia, American technical advisors try to introduce the latest agricultural techniques to peasants who consult astrologers on when to sow and reap, and who believe success with crops or anything else depends on the size of sins they committed in a previous existence. In Manila, the modern-minded capital of the Philippines, it is possible to leave an air-conditioned house complete with television set and electric kitchen, get into a Chevrolet or Buick and after a day's drive over a modern highway reach the mountains of Northern Luzon, where primitive tribes still use spears and poisoned arrows, go about almost naked and raid the lowlands to kill and take human heads. In fact, a great variety of tribal groups, with fascinating customs and handicrafts but backward superstitions and ways of life, inhabit the mountains and jungles of all Southeast Asian countries. They contrast sharply with the semi-Westernized governments which generally scorn and neglect them.

Mostly since World War II, big cities with populations of more than one million, such as Bangkok, Manila, Saigon, Singapore and Jakarta, have developed into modern metropolises with many of the characteristics and problems of huge urban areas all over the world. Many more people than can be accommodated have crowded into these cities, just as in larger cities in Europe and the United States. As elsewhere, dismal slums result, with whole families packed into dirty one-room or two-room shacks lining muddy alleys strewn with rotting garbage.

These conditions breed sickness. As late as 1963 and 1964 cholera—a dreadful disease bred in filth and poverty—flared in Bangkok, Manila and Saigon. The slums breed crime, too. From them come juvenile delinquents who attack and rob unwary tourists, round up customers for prostitutes and gambling dens, fight gang wars and peddle opium and heroin, often becoming addicts themselves.

Hard by the slums stand the resplendent homes of the well-to-do, symbolizing the extreme wealth alongside desperate poverty that has long characterized Southeast Asia. A fairly new phenomenon, however, is the growth of city suburbs, pushing out into the countryside, where the modern houses more and more resemble those in American cities like Miami and Phoenix.

Downtown in the big Southeast Asian cities the streets, in some cases originally nothing more than paths carved out by elephants, water buffaloes or peasants, are now frustratingly inadequate to handle today's heavy traffic. Through these streets throng all manner of pedestrians, including unwary sightseeing villagers and men carrying trays of steaming food over their heads. Maneuvering through the masses of people are bicycles, private cars, madly driven taxis and pedicabs.   63386

One can estimate the state of economic development in a Southeast Asian country by noting the proportionate number of these various vehicles on the city streets. In backward Indonesia, for instance, Jakarta makes do largely with shabby *betchas* (pedicabs), supplemented by a few taxis and an odd collection of rundown buses. Traffic also moves on the smelly, garbage-filled canals built long ago by the Dutch and still used for bathing and the washing of clothes.

Not long ago Bangkok had a network of scenic canals, bustling with little boats and dotted with lotus. In the last 10 years these canals have been covered over and paved; today's wide avenues, less exotic but more efficient, reflect Bangkok's increasing progress and prosperity in the last decade. Rangoon, Burma's capital, relies heavily on pedicabs; Singapore and Saigon have largely passed that stage; and the Philippines hurdled it nearly half a century ago by changing from pony carts to motor vehicles.

Of course, the big Southeast Asian cities have more in common than just slums, juvenile delinquency, traffic jams, increasingly Westernized architecture and enormous billboards advertising American movies. Each city has a large population of Chinese people. Their industriousness, near monopoly of retail trade and continuing *Chineseness* arouse suspicion, envy, resentment and often unfair treat-

ment. In the large towns the Chinese quarter generally boasts incense-filled temples; bustling thorough-
fares; noisy restaurants patronized by people of all
races; food stalls displaying specialized dishes; and
shops selling rice in huge white mounds, ancient
medicines from sea urchins to powdered rhinoceros
horn, whole flattened ducks, dried fish and an as-
sortment of unidentifiable animal entrails.

In most of the large cities there are also officials
and intellectuals whose outlooks are dominated by
intense nationalism and the resentments acquired
under colonialism. The extent of this attitude varies
from place to place; it is bitterly extreme in Jakarta
but hardly noticeable in Kuala Lumpur, the capital
of Malaysia.

Each Southeast Asian city has a very strong personality of its own. Saigon and Rangoon are probably less similar than London and Florence. Part of
each city's special character comes from the linger-
ing influence of its former colonial rulers. A visitor
to Saigon immediately senses a strong French flavor
in the wide, tree-lined boulevards, the stylish shops,
the poor coffee and delicious rich rolls, and the little
restaurants with Parisian food and fine imported
wines. Rangoon's principal hotel still serves its
guests sad British-style food—boiled whitefish with
a slightly soiled-looking white sauce, boiled white
potatoes and brussels sprouts pale and soggy from
seemingly endless cooking.

Though Singapore is probably the most cosmopolitan city in the whole area—with a great variety of Asians, Europeans and Americans—it is still quite British. A number of governmental and other buildings bear the stamp of the Victorian era, department stores are stodgy, and drugstores—always called pharmacies—label bottles of medicine "The Mixture."

Bangkok, which never experienced colonial rule, has a flavor all its own. Gaiety and the spirit of *mai beñ nai* (never mind, it can't be helped) are two of its chief elements.

This, then, is Southeast Asia, from its big cities to its little villages, from the mountain peaks of northern Burma down through the palm-fringed beaches of Sumatra—primitive and modern, changeless and changing, savage and gentle, grim and gay, old and new. No other region of the world is more varied, more fascinating or more challenging.

IV

Pagodas, Palaces and Shrines

OVER MOST of Southeast Asia, religion is an important part of life, affecting and often motivating architecture, painting, music, dancing, harvest celebrations, festivals and everyday habits and attitudes.

In Bangkok an ornate little temple in the Grand Palace houses the most worshipped object in Thailand—the Emerald Buddha, which the Thais took as war booty from the Laotians several centuries ago. It is an image about two feet high, seated aloft on a gilded throne, and its garments are reverently and ceremoniously changed four times a year. "His Majesty the King," said a newspaper at the time of one of my visits to Bangkok, "will proceed to the Chapel Royal of the Emerald Buddha on March 9 to change the robes of the Emerald Buddha for the hot season."

Laos has its own special Buddha image in a temple patronized by the king, in his picturesque little royal capital of Luang Prabang. When Communist-led Pathet Lao troops threatened to capture Luang Prabang in 1961, no amount of persuasion would induce King Savang Vatthana to leave for the safety of Vientiane, the political capital. He unquestioningly accepted the traditional Laotian belief that Buddha gave complete protection to Luang Prabang. His faith was justified. The Pathet Lao troops withdrew.

In Thailand, Burma, Laos and Cambodia the values, rules and practices of Buddhism far outshadow any past or present European influences. One can see yellow-robed Buddhist monks, with shaven heads and calm faces, wandering in the morning through crowded city streets and dusty or muddy lanes with their begging bowls to collect the day's food from men and women who consider it an honor to feed them.

In this region it is still the custom for every young man to spend a period as a monk in a temple. A common sight in Bangkok is a little procession of pedicabs carrying one of these monks-to-be and such gifts from friends as are allowed in temples—alarm clocks, Thermos jugs, a big black parasol.

The modest and respected young King Phumiphon
Aduldet of Thailand spent a month in a monastery,
begging daily like any commoner. Prince Norodom
Sihanouk of Cambodia, who likes to play the saxo-
phone and dance all night, once shaved his royal
head, put on the yellow robes and spent three
months as a novice in the silver-floored palace temple. A quarrel in recent years between the Cambodians and the Thais, historic enemies, over a small
slice of border territory was greatly inflamed by the
fact that the area was the site of a Buddhist temple.

Besides rituals, colorful festivals, little daily rites
and religion-based ceremonies such as the priestly
blessing of a new shop or home, the very landscapes
of Burma, Thailand, Laos and Cambodia testify to
the presence of Buddhism. In Burma, for instance,
there are still more than 2,000 temples in the former capital city Pagan. Monasteries, pagodas and
gilded temples abound in city, town, village and
countryside; a man acquires virtue by building them
or placing gold leaf on them. Statues of Buddha in
all sizes and poses—standing, sitting, lying down—
are everywhere. Greatest and most famous of all
these religious structures is in the heart of Rangoon
—the huge 368-foot gold- and jewel-covered Shwe
Dagon Pagoda, the Holy of Holies to Burmese Buddhists.

If oil-rich little Brunei on Borneo boasts Southeast Asia's most lavish 20th-century Moslem

mosque, Burma certainly can claim the most expensive modern Buddhist structure. U Nu, a devout Buddhist and Premier of Burma for 10 years after it gained independence, built a tremendous new religious center outside Rangoon. It includes dormitories for several thousand monks and scholars, great halls, pagodas (one of them was named the International Peace Pagoda) and a huge artificial hill of concrete honeycombed with air-conditioned caves to resemble the caves in which early Buddhist holy men meditated. The Premier's political enemies charged that he used so much imported cement to build this mammoth and inartistic structure that Burma's post-World War II reconstruction was set back a full year. However, the center does draw Buddhist scholars from all over Asia to study and reinterpret the Buddhist scriptures.

Many Vietnamese are ardent Roman Catholics, and great European-style cathedrals still tower over the Communist-ruled countryside of North Vietnam. In the Christian Philippines the morning procession is made up not of monks with begging bowls but of whole families, the women covering their heads with black shawls, trooping to mass. Soft red stone temples with statues of Hindu gods and carvings and paintings depicting portions of the Ramayana, the great epic poem of ancient India, symbolize the integration of Balinese life around Hinduism.

Except for the Hindu Balinese and groups of

Christians like the Ambonese, Minadonese and Bataks, Indonesia is Moslem. There—as among the Moslem Malays of Malaysia—the Friday call to prayers empties homes and government offices and fills the streets with mosque-bound throngs. Although the tropics seem to have somewhat softened the strictness of their religion, these Indonesians and Malaysians observe the daytime fasting of the sacred month of Ramadan (the ninth month of the Mohammedan calendar year) and hope someday to make the pilgrimage to Mecca.

Though they worship the Moslem Allah (God), Indonesians still cling to many Hindu-Buddhist symbols and attitudes from the early pre-Moslem period. Indonesian dances are built around tales of Hindu gods. The Garuda, an Indonesian national symbol, is a mythical Hindu bird. In Indonesian thinking, mystic Hindu strains run deep, especially in the central island of Java. And Indonesian women are not barred from mosques or forced to wear veils as is the case in other parts of the Moslem world.

Perhaps partly because they retain Hindu traits, these days Indonesians emphatically assert their Moslem character in many ways. For example, they have begun to build their mosques not with traditional Indonesian-style roofs but with domes as in the Middle East.

Vietnamese traditional architecture employs the upswept Chinese roof. Long ago Vietnamese emperors built their capital, Hue, on the Chinese pattern, and about a century and a half ago they constructed there an exact though smaller replica of the magnificent imperial Forbidden City in Peking. I first visited Hue in 1952, just after the Communist-led Vietminh, rebelling against the French, had razed almost every one of the royal buildings, laying waste in a useless orgy of destruction one of their country's great heritages.

As I stood there that day in 1952, imaginatively reconstructing Hue from a few remaining landmarks and my sharp recollections of Peking, I suddenly remembered watching eight years earlier the devastation of the Royal Palaces of Mandalay, built not in the Chinese but in the India-oriented Buddhist style. The Japanese had chosen to make their last stand in the walled royal compound of Mandalay, the ancient capital of Burma, uninhabited since the British had deposed King Thibaw, the country's degenerate last monarch. The British shelled it. The history-laden palaces, flamboyantly painted structures with soaring spires, steep gold roofs, massive lacquered pillars and richly ornamented furnishings, went up in flames. Today only gilded temples and stupas still echo something of the glitter and grandeur that was Mandalay.

To the delight of tourists, Bangkok's brilliant palaces, fashioned in Thailand's sophisticated, airy and almost tinselly style, remain intact. King Phumi-

phon Aduldet has avoided living in the Chakri
Grand Palace of his forefathers because his brother,
the former King Ananda Mahidol, was murdered
there by an assassin who has evaded discovery for
more than 15 years. But King Phumiphon comes to
the towering building with the characteristic Thai
gold-tiled roof for certain ceremonial occasions.
One was the elaborate cremation of his royal
brother. A magnificent and massive procession of
mourners on foot—the King, his relatives, courtiers,
officials in splendid traditional dress, officers in full
uniform, Brahmin priests, orange-robed monks, foreign diplomats and dignitaries in formal array—and
gilded carriages bearing the royal golden urn and
other sacred utensils and ornaments took three
hours under the burning sun to negotiate the half
mile from the palace to the towering cremation
pavilion, which after proper rites was set ablaze
to consume Ananda Mahidol's body.

The great stone temples and palaces of Angkor,
wreathed in jungle in a sparsely populated section of
Cambodia, still stand as a testament to the splendid
Khmer Empire. A thousand miles to the south, near
Jogjakarta in Java, the great many-tiered temple
pyramid of Borobudur, covered with intricately
carved stone blocks illustrating episodes in the life
of the Buddha, provides another stupendous example of the same period of great Southeast Asian
builders. In central Burma's holy city of Pagan,

founded in the ninth century, the 2,190 separate
spire-topped shrines cover 25 square miles of countryside in a spectacular if haphazard tribute to Lord
Buddha. The central shrine, the gilded cylindrical
Shwezigon, is supposed to contain one of Buddha's
teeth.

During the time they ruled Cambodia the French
rescued the monumental temples and palaces of
Angkor from the greedy jungle and reconstructed
them by a painstaking process called anastolysis.
This involves taking a huge crumbling structure
apart, stone by stone, numbering each one and then
placing it back exactly in its original position. The
Dutch used the same slow and exacting method with
Borobudur, Prembanan and the Madjopahit ruins
outside Surabaya. In recent years John D. Rockefel-
ler III has helped finance plans for preserving Pagan's stupas.

Independent Cambodia is attempting to keep up
the work of the French at Angkor. Laos has renewed her more important temples. In Manila the
authorities have rebuilt much of the old Spanish
walled city, Intramuros, where the beautiful cathe-
dral and old Spanish palaces were destroyed in the
fighting during World War II.

In Bangkok there is an excellent museum con-
taining the best of Thailand's traditional paintings,
sculpture and pottery. The Thai government, like a
good many others in Asia, tries to keep foreign col-

lectors and museums from buying and making off with its more important pieces of art. It has ruled that any art object taken out of Thailand must have on it the stamp of the museum and a museum tag stating that the plate, Buddha head or whatever is not a national treasure.

All the Southeast Asian countries are officially fostering their traditional dances. The Cambodian court maintains a dance troupe that trains regularly under the stern and expert supervision of a wrinkled old ballet mistress in an open-air pavilion on the grounds of Prince Norodom Sihanouk's palace. The Bayanihan Filipino troupe has preserved traditional Philippine dánces and performs them brilliantly on world tours.

James Thompson, an American who has built a famous and important national industry by reviving Thai-Laotian home-loom silk weaving, has made the Thais more conscious of the beauty of their teak houses by combining three of these for his home and filling it with lovingly collected Thai art objects.

So, amid the rush of modernization, individuals and governments are making efforts to preserve Southeast Asia's magnificent cultural heritage. This heritage is inextricably intertwined with religion, and for most Southeast Asians, whether Buddhist, Moslem, Catholic or animist, religion, as we have said, is a very meaningful and integral part of life.

V

Independence: The Influence of Heritage and of Leaders

ON JULY 4, 1946, hundreds of thousands of enthusiastic Filipinos gathered on the Luneta, a large grassy parade ground fronting the sea at Manila, to witness ceremonies celebrating their country's birth as an independent republic. President Manuel Roxas and United States officials delivered emotional speeches. The Stars and Stripes was lowered and the flag of the Philippines was raised. For the Filipinos the occasion brought to an end 385 years of colonial rule—the first 337 years under Spain and the last 48 years under the United States. For Southeast Asia a course was set that was to be followed by all the other colonial powers.

In 1947 the British granted independence to Burma. The Netherlands withdrew from Indonesia in 1949; the French from Vietnam, Cambodia and Laos by 1954; the British from Malaya by 1957; and from Singapore and the Borneo territories of Sarawak and Sabah by 1963.

Independence, hailed by the peoples of Southeast Asia with fiery enthusiasm and great expectation, has brought not only the satisfactions of national self-determination but also turmoil and bitterness, problems and woes. Two decades after that momentous day on the Luneta the Southeast Asian nations are still struggling to develop stable governments, to cope with internal divisions and outside threats, to achieve greater economic development and to create modern societies. Some of these nations show little progress; others have been reasonably successful. For most of the region the prospects are uncertain.

Why have some nations done well and others poorly? There are a number of reasons. Some were handicapped to begin with by conditions that existed prior to independence, and some by the circumstances in which they achieved independence. Some have been disrupted by domestic and foreign Communists, and some menaced by neighboring countries. Religious and racial minorities have been a problem in most countries of Southeast Asia and a threat to survival in some. Ideological confusion and rivalries, clashes between ambitious and irresponsible leaders and groups, illiteracy, poverty, population pressure and shortages of material resources and trained personnel have been serious obstacles in some countries, less serious in others.

World War II spread misery and destruction throughout Southeast Asia. Thus, peoples facing independence had to cope not only with all the problems of self-rule but also with war damage that aggravated poverty and general economic backwardness. In addition, economies that had been developed to provide raw materials for colonial powers were serious obstacles to nations determined to be economically as well as politically independent.

Most Southeast Asians entered the postwar period leaning toward the liberal democratic political systems of their former rulers who had won the war. But they were influenced not only by European and American ideas of human rights, freedom and democratic government but also by Marxism. The Soviet Union, it must be remembered, had been on the side of the victors, and during World War II the Allies had cooperated with Communist movements, including some guerrilla groups in Southeast Asia. Moreover, Communism in China had emerged from the war with powerful momentum, emphasizing strong nationalism and proclaiming a so-called "new democracy" along with Marxist ideas. Even in many quarters in the West the Socialist brand of Marxism—and to some extent the Communist form —was regarded as progressive and somehow better than capitalist democracy.

So in building what they hoped would be their brave new independent world some Southeast Asians favored full Communism; some a middle democratic-Socialist way; and some, notably those who took over in the Philippines and Malaysia, Western-style democracy. Within each country those who chose Communism became bitter opponents of those who did not. In the northern half of Vietnam those who worked for Communism came to power as an internationally recognized government. In neighboring Laos, Communists control more than half the country, though their regime is not internationally recognized as legitimate.

Except in the area of Vietnam where the Communists gained control, all the former colonies of Southeast Asia tried some form of democratic government after they gained independence. Most failed to make a go of it. The reasons were many and varied. But it is significant that those countries whose leaders were strongly influenced by Marxist ideology failed with the democratic system. In the Philippines and Malaysia, where the leaders had a non-Marxist attitude, the democratic system has so far succeeded. In Burma and Indonesia, where Marxist ideas had a strong grip, the collapse of attempts at democracy with a Socialist flavoring led to a drift into authoritarian systems in which individual liberty gave way to the central authority of the government.

It is also significant that those countries which abstained from dogmatic Socialist and Communist systems and which maintained cooperative economic and political relations with the West have been more stable, prosperous and progressive than those which have gone the Socialist or Communist way and are internationally oriented toward the Communist powers.

In all the Southeast Asian countries as they reached the point of independence, leadership was for the most part in the hands of intellectuals, who were generally from families that had been able to afford to educate them. These passionately nationalistic and anticolonialist patriots had studied at the high schools or universities of their colonial rulers and had learned the political concepts of Western societies. Even though these leaders had the support of the masses, they often had no close identity with them and had very little understanding of their needs and attitudes.

Typical of these men who gave the early intellectual leadership to independence movements were Sutan Sjarir in Indonesia, U Nu in Burma and Son Ngoc Thanh in Cambodia. All were moderate Socialists but also humanists and democrats; they were products of both the East and the West. After independence was won, however, they and most others like them were pushed aside by less honest, tougher and more selfishly ambitious leaders.

On frequent visits to Indonesia since 1950 I have sat with Sjarir for hours on his front veranda in Jakarta. A relaxed, chunky, bright-eyed man, Sjarir was once Indonesia's Premier, and we discussed why moderates like himself lost influence in the post-independence era. Clearly, a big reason was that this group rejected the ruthless methods, the inflaming of anti-Western passions and the personal gains typical of those who were getting ahead. On a visit to Jakarta in 1963 I was unable to see Sjarir. He had been imprisoned by Sukarno, his old revolutionary associate, who had become dictator of Indonesia by using the tactics that Sjarir eschewed.

Sukarno's role in Indonesia illustrates how the characters and ambitions of Southeast Asia's leaders have shaped their countries. Indonesia, for example, would not be what it is today but for Sukarno—that vain, handsome, unscrupulous, charming politician who is so fond of pomp and power, so susceptible to flattery, so incapable of viewing either himself or his national problems objectively. His urge to be a medieval sultan in the 20th century has kept him maneuvering—successfully—through the shifting intrigues of both Indonesian politics and the cold war. Sukarno still retains all his capacity to stir the Indonesian masses for whom he does so little.

Through appeals to nationalist passions, bold and astute manipulation of political forces and the use of slick slogans to express crude and oversimplified Socialist concepts, he has maintained a personal domination over a weak but swashbuckling and expansionist Indonesia that makes a Western observer think automatically of Mussolini and Fascist Italy.

Similarly, in Cambodia the personal impulses of short, plump, ebullient and emotional Norodom Sihanouk have largely determined the course of that country. Prince (formerly King) Norodom Sihanouk, the Premier and Chief of State, is a humane, sensitive and patriotic aristocrat with a real concern for the welfare of his people. At the same time he is an Asian ex-monarch operating on the theory that he has a "divine right" to determine Cambodia's destiny and the obligation to cast his country's traditional enemies into oblivion. Like Sukarno, he uses his tremendous personal appeal to consolidate a personal and, on the whole, benevolent dictatorship.

In Burma the gentle and extremely devout Buddhist U Nu symbolized and guided his war-ravaged, rather happy-go-lucky and inefficient country. That Burma took a road sharply different from the one U Nu planned was due to another Asian strongman, General Ne Win (an adopted political name meaning "Brilliant as the Sun"). A husky, hot-tempered, quick-witted but not markedly intelligent martinet who is driven as much by a strong taste for discipline as by personal ambition, Ne Win, about ten years younger than Sukarno and a decade older than Sihanouk, is determined to put Burma into some kind of trim, orderly condition. Though a poor second to the likes of Sukarno and Sihanouk in personal magnetism and crowd appeal, Ne Win possesses affability and charm. However, he scorns to use them to win public popularity and he regards the type of Socialism he practices as a means mostly of organizing and controlling Burmese society rather than of developing it to meet the challenge of a radically changing world.

The recent evolution of the Philippines is also partly due to the character of its leaders. For example, Ramon Magsaysay, who was President from 1953 until his tragic death in a plane crash in 1957, probably saved his country's democracy by tackling a strong Communist rebellion, economic chaos and official corruption. A man of humble background who had operated a small fleet of buses and looked like a middleweight boxer, Magsaysay was elected because of a quality that is all too rare in Asia: he really cared about the "little" man and went to city slums and hundreds of tiny peasant communities to say so. Probably at some cost to efficiency, he opened the luxurious Presidential Palace at Malacanang to all Filipinos, however poor or shabby. He worked hard at cleaning up the graft and corrupt rule by privileged cliques that were undermining the government. By economic and social reforms, military force and the ability to welcome and follow Western advice he smashed the Communists who were threatening to seize control of the Philippines.

Present Philippine President Diosdado Macapagal, though more austere and intellectual than Magsaysay, has a similar dedication to the people and a down-to-earth approach to national problems. He has exerted himself to bring new economic freedoms and official honesty into Philippine affairs.

In Thailand, which might well be included here though not a former colony, it was a professional soldier, Field Marshal Sarit Thanarat, burly, convivial and unsophisticated but tough, practical-minded and shrewd, who in 1957 ended a costly comic-opera sequence of military coups and established, at least for a time, sufficient stability for economic development.

In South Vietnam the stubborn courage of Ngo Dinh Diem, a devout Roman Catholic, was responsible for such stability as existed. But his aloof and authoritarian approach, his inability to communicate with his co-workers or his people, and his unquestioning reliance on corrupt relatives alienated his support, led to his downfall and death and brought about the political disorder that followed.

In Malaysia it was Tunku (Prince) Abdul Rahman—an affable, relaxed, warmhearted and witty Malay aristocrat who likes golf, racing, cigars,

poker and even his nation's former British ruler—
who persuaded the fractious communities of Chinese, Malays, Indians, Kedazans, Ibans, Muruts and
others to cooperate enough to bring Malaysia into
existence. And it is the Tunku who has kept the
Federation of Malaysia stable, in spite of Singapore's
departure and threats and guerrilla invasions directed
by Sukarno.

In Laos another aristocrat, Prince Souvanna
Phouma, has had the suppleness and patience to
deal with the disparate and often feuding non-
Communist elements in his part of the country,
thereby helping to save at least some of Laos from
the Communist domination that is led by his half-
brother, Prince Souphanouvong.

VI

Independence: What Self-Rule Has Wrought

Two Southeast Asian countries, the Philippines and Malaysia, are examples of an attempt to maintain a democratic way of life. Both attained independence under comparably favorable circumstances and both have since been aided extensively by their former colonial rulers, the United States and Britain. But they have also benefited from a relatively free democratic political and economic system.

As a former colony itself, the United States assuaged its qualms of conscience for taking over the Philippines in 1893 by adopting a liberal policy directly aimed at eventual independence. Indeed, any other policy would have required brutal repression, because the Filipinos had already sought independence from Spain through revolt. Filipinos accepted

American rule on the condition that it was a guardianship of limited duration.

The United States fostered representative government through free elections and appointed Filipinos to administrative and judicial positions at all levels. As early as 1907 Filipinos elected the lower house of the National Assembly; this was the first elected legislative body in all Southeast Asia. By 1913 there was a Filipino majority in the upper house. The American governor-general still retained veto powers and other controls, but these were steadily curtailed. By 1935 the Philippines had become a commonwealth, with full internal self-government under its own President, Manuel Quezon.

The United States also developed education on a wide scale. English was used in primary schools and became the common language of many Filipinos. In 1936 the United States promised the Philippines independence in 10 years and, even though World War II intervened, kept its promise.

Of course, there were some bad aspects of the American record in the Philippines. The United States failed to relieve the peasants who were oppressed tenants on the great landed estates formed under the Spanish. This absence of land reform left the country a legacy of agricultural backwardness and acute social and political problems. In addition, independence agreements whereby American business interests acquired special privileges in the ex-colony after its independence caused ill feeling.

Fortunately, later United States policy alleviated the effects of these mistakes. Of prime importance was the massive economic aid the United States provided—$2 billion in the first five years of Philippine independence—to reconstruct the war-torn country. In addition, the military assistance the United States furnished to build up the Philippine armed forces helped the government to defeat the Communist uprisings.

Since independence the 32 million people of the Philippines, who live in an area of 116,000 square miles, have had an elected, presidential rule. It has been flawed by corruption and too often has served as the instrument of the privileged classes, but nevertheless it functions with considerable effectiveness. The verdict of the ballot box is respected, and power is transferred peacefully from one president, and one political party, to another. Filipinos enjoy free speech, free assembly and other basic civil rights. Manila's international and domestic policy is anti-Communist, and the Philippines is an ally of the United States.

Free enterprise, operating within the framework of national planning and government control, has figured prominently in maintaining for the Philippines an average annual economic growth of 6 per

cent between 1954 and 1964. Average annual income by 1962 had reached $200 per person, second
only to Malaysia's in Southeast Asia.

Malaysia, composed of many different peoples—
10.8 million in an area of more than 128,000
square miles—is a federation that has still to unite
itself as a nation. Nevertheless, its members—
originally Malaya, Singapore and the Borneo territories of Sarawak and Sabah—have shown considerable political maturity; their record is one of relative
progress so far. After two years in the federation
Singapore withdrew, but as a separate unit has continued with a relatively free, democratic system.

Before World War II the British, who ruled these
colonies that have now combined to form Malaysia,
did not foresee independence. They kept top-level
administration in their own hands. However, they
did much to develop education, economic welfare,
public services and the rule of law.

After the war ended with the defeat of Japan the
British resumed control of their colonies, but they
committed themselves to an eventual grant of independence. They began to encourage free political
activity. They held elections and put local people in
government posts. For a decade, however, political
progress had to take second place to the task of sup-
pressing a highly dangerous Communist uprising,
strongest and most threatening in Malaya and Sin-

gapore. Moreover, Britain faced great difficulty in settling differences between more than 4 million Chinese people of immigrant stock with no pronounced religious feelings, nearly 4 million strongly Moslem Malays, some 900,000 resident Hindu and Moslem Indians and Pakistanis, and about 700,000 Borneo peoples of various kinds, who lived in the territories which were to become Malaysia.

However, responsible Malay, Chinese and Indian leaders showed the way in Malaya, easily the most important unit in the future state, by submerging the rivalries of their three groups in a big Alliance Party that led the colony to independence in 1957. With the Alliance gaining large electoral majorities and proving to be a strong stabilizing force, Malaya's democratic system had displayed an ability to function effectively, maintain basic freedoms and foster economic growth. A state-supervised, free-enterprise economy has shown a growth rate slightly better than that of the Philippines in recent years.

Singapore and the Borneo territories of Sarawak and Sabah became independent in 1963 by merging with Malaya to form the new nation of Malaysia. The little oil-rich British protectorate of Brunei in northern Borneo chose not to join the federation. As in Malaya, democracy has functioned with reasonable success in the Borneo sections of Malaysia and in Singapore.

Malaysia, whose foreign policy is anti-Communist

and pro-West, has remained in the British Commonwealth and maintains close ties with Britain, including a defense alliance. Even guerrilla aggression
from Indonesia has failed to disrupt Malaysia's
democratic system. Malaysia is a constitutional
monarchy, the king being elected for a fixed term
by the sultans of the nine Malay states of Malaya, who rotate the kingship among themselves.
However, the government is headed by a prime minister—Tunku Abdul Rahman, at this writing. When
Lee Kuan Yew, the Premier of Singapore, in 1965
began to agitate for greater rights for the Chinese in
the federation, the result was a hostile and apprehen-
sive Malay reaction that eventually led to Singapore's
withdrawal under pressure from Malay leaders. Singapore became a small, independent island state, but
maintained close defense and economic ties with
Malaysia.

In a different category from the Philippines and
Malaysia are Burma, Indonesia and Cambodia. All
started out after independence with liberal democratic but Socialist-oriented systems. All later turned
to authoritarianism within a Marxist framework and
all practice a Communist-leaning neutralism in international affairs.

The record of British rule in Burma—which with
an area of 262,000 square miles is the largest Southeast Asian country after Indonesia—is similar to

that in Malaya, Singapore and Borneo. However, the Burmese grew restive at the slowness of the British in giving them self-government and, as a result, their independence movement developed before World War II and allied itself with the invading Japanese. After winning Burma from the British, the Japanese set up a puppet government, naming a number of independence leaders to cabinet posts. However, when the Burmese nationalists found they had no real self-government under the Japanese, they helped Britain reconquer their land. After the war Britain accepted independence as the goal for Burma and on January 4, 1948, yielded sovereignty to a newly elected Burmese government. Unlike Malaysia, Burma chose to leave the British Commonwealth.

Burmese independence did not begin auspiciously, despite the fact that astrologers had named the date and hour for the new government's start. Six months before the transfer of sovereignty a gang of political rivals assassinated Aung San, revered leader of the independence movement, along with six other prominent nationalists. The post of premier, which had been reserved for him in the new government, was taken by U Nu, who was a close colleague of Aung San. U Nu was quickly faced with a crisis. The Karens, a largely Christian minority, rebelled when denied wide self-rule. The Communists revolted at the same time. The government's struggle against these and other discontented minorities—the Shans, Kachins and Mons—who later arose in scattered outbreaks sapped its energies for years. By 1964 the government had greatly reduced but still not eliminated rebel activity.

Social and economic progress in Burma has been hampered by the disruptions caused by the uprisings, by the overly doctrinaire Socialist bent of the government and its inexperience and inefficiency, and by strains over long-time monopoly of business and trade by immigrant Chinese and Indians. Reflecting national frustration, General Ne Win, the quick-to-anger commander of the armed forces, seized power in March, 1962, abolished the democratic constitution, imprisoned U Nu and hundreds of other political leaders without trial and established a military regime. Since then Ne Win's Revolutionary Council has embarked on a drastic program called "the Burmese Way to Socialism" under which it has suppressed most civil liberties; taken over virtually all private enterprise, domestic- and foreign-owned; and regimented most phases of national life.

The General has terminated cultural contacts with the West and private Western assistance programs, and has pursued a policy of extreme political isolation and neutralism. Ne Win's Burma displays an unfriendly aloofness toward the West and an outwardly friendly but basically suspicious and fearful

attitude toward Communist China. Meanwhile Ne
Win's regime has made even less headway than did
U Nu's in advancing Burma's social and economic
development. In 1965 production was still lower
than before World War II for a population, now
about 25 million, that has grown by more than a
third in the last 20 years.

Indonesia is Southeast Asia's largest country,
with a population of over 100 million and an area of
735,000 square miles including approximately
3,000 islands. Developments there have basically
followed the Burmese pattern. Before World War II
Indonesia—then a colony called the Dutch East
Indies—possessed only limited political rights and
educational advantages. Thus, when independence
came, the Indonesians were perhaps the least prepared of all the Southeast Asian peoples in terms
of training and experience for the tasks of self-
government.

Before independence, nationalist and Communist
movements developed. But the Dutch suppressed
them and imprisoned their leaders. At first, therefore, Indonesians welcomed the Japanese wartime
occupation, but later turned against the Japanese
because of their harsh policies. Shortly before the
end of the war the Japanese, foreseeing defeat,
sponsored an Independence Preparatory Committee
of Indonesians. Two days after the Japanese sur-

render the Committee proclaimed the independent Republic of Indonesia, with Sukarno as President.

When the Dutch returned after the war, they planned greater self-government for Indonesia but continued association with the Netherlands. The Indonesians resisted re-establishment of Dutch domination, and years of periodic fighting followed. Finally, weary of the struggle, the Dutch recognized Indonesia's independence in late 1949.

Like the Burmese, the Indonesians set up a government that was liberal democratic in principle but had strong socialist tendencies at home and neutralist ones abroad. This regime turned out to be unbelievably inefficient. It saddled the country's people and economy with all kinds of rigid state controls. It proved unfriendly to foreign investment and to private businessmen, who were mostly Chinese and Dutch. There were frequent changes of government as rival political parties, ranging from conservative Moslem through moderate Socialist to Communist, schemed for power. Economic and social conditions fell apart rapidly. Corruption and rising prices became worse. The first popular elections, held in 1955, failed to bring improvement. Rebellion by a fanatical Moslem faction, the Darul Islam, and scattered uprisings by other groups weakened the regime.

Although under the constitution the President had no executive authority, Sukarno started to exert more influence, using his appeal to the masses to increase his power. He began more and more to favor the most emotional nationalists and the Communists. They in turn found they could greatly improve their positions by flattering Sukarno and cooperating with him. The Communist Party expanded rapidly to become the largest in the country while the moderate Socialist and Moslem parties found themselves pushed into a secondary status. In 1958 prominent Moslem leaders and a number of Socialists and military commanders in Sumatra, Celebes and Indonesian Borneo revolted and formed a separate government in Padang, West Sumatra. The bulk of the Indonesian armed forces proved loyal to Sukarno, however, and crushed the revolt.

Amid continuing social and economic deterioration after the revolt President Sukarno and his followers decided the time had come to dispense with parliamentary democracy. In 1959 Sukarno moved to consolidate his personal power by dissolving the parliament, postponing scheduled elections and appointing a rubber-stamp "mutual help" legislature divided between presidentially favored parties and "functional" groups. The set-up was to be "guided democracy."

By discarding the legal constitution and reinstating the provisional constitution of 1945, Sukarno made himself chief executive in fact as well as in name. He became premier as well as president, and later he had himself named president for life. An emotional and noisy campaign forced the Netherlands to turn over to Indonesia the territory of West New Guinea (now West Irian), which the Dutch had continued to occupy after recognizing Indonesian independence. The campaign proved useful in generating emotion inside Indonesia and therefore furthered support for the Sukarno regime.

Sukarno now presides over an authoritarian government that combines Communists, nationalists, military men and Moslem conservatives—some of whose leaders Sukarno has imprisoned. The regime has nationalized the major part of the economy and taken over most foreign-owned properties and businesses. The only surviving newspapers are government-controlled. The government has transformed the big companies that produce and refine Indonesia's oil into state enterprises and has put their British and American managements under Indonesian supervision and control. With his hold on the population still effective, Sukarno is a complete dictator in a system that claims to be building "Socialism à la Indonesia."

The Communist Party is a powerful faction in the regime, but so far the armed forces have been strong enough to check any Communist move to take over. Meanwhile in what could be the richest nation in Southeast Asia the state-managed economy declines steadily, wild inflation has made the currency prac-

tically worthless and the standard of living is one of
the lowest in the world—annual per-capita income
being estimated at about $55. Life expectancy is
about 32 years, and people who complain they have
no rice to eat have been told they can eat rats.

Increasingly anti-Western, Sukarno's Indonesia
used Malaysia's close ties with Britain as justification for proclaiming in 1963 a policy of "crushing"
the new state, which Sukarno maintained was "neo-
colonialist"—practically a British colony. Indonesia
has smuggled guerrillas into Malaysia and concen-
trated troops along the Indonesian-Malaysian border in Borneo, forcing a defensive gathering of
Malaysian and British Commonwealth forces. When
Malaysia was named a temporary member of the
United Nations Security Council, Indonesia noisily
withdrew from the United Nations. Sukarno spurns
American assistance ("To hell with U.S. aid," he
shouts at the crowds), regularly denounces liberal
democracy as "the disease of parties, parties, parties" and equates the West with imperialism. His regime maintains close ties with Communist China
and has made arrangements to accept financial help
and "military experience" from that country.

The little kingdom of Cambodia, which has the
smallest area of any state in Southeast Asia—
67,000 square miles, about the size of Missouri
—and a population of 6 million, provides a more

successful example than Indonesia of Marxist-influenced authoritarian development. Before World War II, French rule rested lightly on Cambodia because of its minor political and economic importance. The kingdom had the status of a protectorate and retained its monarch and other traditional institutions.

Near the end of the war the Japanese occupiers of Cambodia, sensing defeat by the Allies, approved the formation of an independent Cambodian government under young King Norodom Sihanouk. Faced with this government when they resumed power in Cambodia, the French agreed to independent government for the country—within the French Union. When this proved to be only a cover-up for continued French rule, some Cambodian Communists and non-Communists rebelled. National Assembly elections were held, with French approval and under a new constitution, and newly elected members promptly demanded complete independence.

In 1953, faced with political attacks because he seemed to be cooperating too much with the French, King Sihanouk acted pretty much as Sukarno later did in Indonesia under different circumstances. He moved out of the purely figurehead role assigned to him by the constitution, declared martial law and dismissed the cabinet and National Assembly. To undermine his critics he staged a campaign for inde-

pendence himself and put such pressures on France
that by the end of 1953 he had gained full sovereignty for his country.

As part of his independence campaign the King
held long interviews, speaking with foreign journalists in fluent French. These interviews created world
sympathy for Cambodia and accounted for a good
deal of the pressure on France. I spent a morning in
Siem Reap, a little town near the great Angkor ruins
in western Cambodia, taking down one of these interviews. And King Sihanouk's followers, getting
the entire text of my story about the interview from
the files of the telegraph office, circulated copies of
it all over Cambodia. Such public statements and
King Sihanouk's other dramatic gestures of defiance
brought a large proportion of former political critics
to his side.

By this time the King, like Sukarno, had decided
he did not want to return to the free elections and
frustrating party rivalries of the former parliamentary system. He engineered the formation of a big
national party called the People's Socialist Community and headed it himself. To have freedom for political activity, he turned the throne over to his father and became Premier as Prince Sihanouk. Since
then he has suppressed opposition. When his father
died Sihanouk got a newly elected National Assembly, controlled by his mass party, to name him chief
of state as well as premier in a kingless monarchy.

These positions gave him full power over all areas of government and legislation. Cambodia has thus become a semi-dictatorship. Like Sukarno, Sihanouk is immensely popular. But, unlike Sukarno, he gives his country reasonably effective government and some economic development.

Borrowing a de Gaulle tactic, Prince Sihanouk calls for national referendums when challenged on critical issues. He always wins. One of his public relations devices is to hold a sort of national town meeting at which he himself presides and answers questions with enjoyment and enthusiasm.

Prince Sihanouk has combined benevolent internal control with state Socialism. He opposes Communism domestically; but largely because of United States ties with South Vietnam and Thailand, Cambodia's traditional enemies, he is friendly with Communist China and hostile to the United States.

Prince Sihanouk's recent moves to nationalize important sectors of the economy may be damaging, but with extensive foreign aid from both East and West, Cambodia has been a relatively prosperous and developing state. So far, despite one revolt which he put down before it got off the ground, the Prince has shown that Socialist-oriented authoritarianism and pro-Communist neutralism do not have to go hand in hand with internal troubles or economic deterioration.

*   *   *

The kingdom of Thailand—with about 31 million people in an area of 198,000 square miles, three times the size of Cambodia—also belongs in the category of Southeast Asian countries that have turned from free, competitive democracy to dictatorship. The only Southeast Asian country that has never been a colony, Thailand (formerly Siam) has pioneered some of the paths of political development the colonialized states later followed. Today it has arrived at a stage of development that cannot be bracketed with that of any other Southeast Asian nation.

Thailand went through a liberal democratic phase in the early nineteen-thirties, well before other lands in the area. Its great kings of the 19th and early 20th centuries had already put Thailand on the road to modernization. While doing so, they avoided the danger of colonialization by yielding slices of territory or by granting special rights to foreigners. Under King Prajadhipok, who ascended the throne in 1925, royal leadership weakened. Resentful of the monarchy's claim to absolute authority, a reform group of civilian officials and military officers, organized as the People's Party, staged a coup in 1932 and forced the King to accept figurehead status under a provisional constitution and a parliament made up of People's Party members.

Conflicting factions developed, and the political instability that followed was to last for two decades.

The coup's leader, Pridi Sanomyong, was forced by opponents within the reform group to leave the country temporarily when he advocated an economic plan that called for nationalization of almost all natural and industrial resources. His scheme, considered and rejected in Thailand 30 years ago, was similar to the Marxist-type programs still preoccupying leaders in Indonesia, Burma and Cambodia today.

Pridi's exile represented a right-wing gain within the coup's forces. Eventually a young colonel named Pibul Songgram took control and instituted an extreme nationalism. King Prajadhipok abdicated and Prince Ananda Mahidol, still only a boy and living in Switzerland, was named Thailand's monarch *in absentia*.

Pibul cooperated with the Japanese during World War II. As Allied victory became certain, he had to yield power to Pridi, who had been leading the anti-Japanese resistance and who acted as regent for the absent young King. Confused factional activities followed, marked by an attempt in 1946 at elected parliamentary government under a new constitution. King Ananda came home that same year to assume the crown, but was promptly assassinated. His younger brother, Phumiphon Aduldet, was named his successor. Out of the intrigues and power rivalries Pibul emerged again as the chief figure in a dictatorial anti-Communist regime until he was overthrown in 1957 by Field Marshal Sarit Thanarat. Pibul went into exile and later died.

With a supporting military group Sarit—a vigorous, jovial man of humble birth—dominated Thailand until his own death in 1963, after which his Deputy Premier, Thanom Kittikachorn, took over. It has since been publicized that Sarit appropriated vast sums from the public funds for private purposes, but he gave the country relatively effective government and enjoyed considerable popularity despite some secret opposition.

Under the dictatorship of Sarit and Thanom, Thailand has shown comparative stability, prosperity and substantial progress in most fields. The kingdom's rate of economic growth under a free-enterprise system has been around 5 per cent a year, exceeded in Southeast Asia only by those of Malaysia and the Philippines. Like Sarit before him, Thanom relies upon the specialized skills of a capable group of permanent civil administrators, thus contributing to the competent handling of government affairs. King Phumiphon, though only a symbolic head of state, is permitted a prominent public rule, and the Thai people like this return to tradition. Thailand, allied with the United States through the Southeast Asia Treaty Organization (SEATO), has been strongly anti-Communist under Sarit and Thanom, as under Pibul. Opposition groups, including Communists, have been sternly suppressed.

* * *

In Vietnam, recent political action has been dominated by Communism and the struggle against it. Before World War II the French developed Vietnam culturally, educationally and economically to a considerable degree, but their limited response to Vietnamese demands for more self-government resulted in periodic rebellions. Communists played a prominent part in the revolutionary activity. Near the end of World War II Emperor Bao Dai, encouraged by the Japanese occupiers of his country, proclaimed Vietnam's independence. Immediately following Japan's defeat, however, he had to give way to a Communist-led government headed by Ho Chi Minh. When the French attempted to re-establish their prewar rule, a bitter eight-year war with Ho's Communist League for Vietnamese Independence (Vietminh) began. The French surrendered in 1954.

Ho Chi Minh—a fragile-looking man with the wispy goatee of a Chinese scholar, expressive eyes and a sensitive and intelligent face—is the oldest living revolutionary leader in Asia. Born a few years before China's Mao Tse-tung, he was already visiting Moscow while the Chinese Communist Party was still in its infancy. Ho held the very important post of director of the whole Far Eastern bureau of the international Communist organization when Mao had not yet achieved leadership of the Chinese

Communist Party. For decades engaged in many forms of revolutionary activity, for decades in hiding and for recent decades a legend, "Uncle Ho" is playing the life-and-death game of Communist revolution with the same cunning, unbeatable persistence and infinite patience he displayed back in the days when Asia's revolutions, Communist or nationalist, were but a distant dream.

I covered the last four years of the war between the Vietminh and the French, so similar to the savage struggle in which Americans are now involved in Vietnam. Ho was with his forces in the caves and jungles of northwestern Vietnam which the French never penetrated. But just after the war I got to see —though not to talk with—this bent, frail little man. He was being cheered in Hanoi, now North Vietnam's capital, as he delivered a fiery speech to a mass meeting outside the drab French-built municipal theater, known as the Opera House.

The international agreements signed in Geneva in 1954 that ended the French-Vietminh struggle recognized Communist control of Vietnam north of the 17th Parallel. South of the Parallel the agreements granted sovereignty to a government in Saigon to which the French had in stages given full independence.

The Hanoi regime has implanted in North Vietnam a full-fledged Communist system which, though oppressive, has effectively organized national energies. Despite some progress in industrialization, the rate of over-all economic growth has not been high and standards of living are still miserably low. In South Vietnam, Ngo Dinh Diem—a strong nationalist but a stubborn, aloof and dictatorial man—was chosen by the French and by Vietnamese leaders to head the government in 1954. He instituted a constitution and won a presidential election in 1955. During its early years South Vietnam showed solid economic gains and general progress. However, after Ho's regime in Hanoi helped start a campaign of guerrilla subversion in the South aimed at overthrowing the South Vietnamese government, Diem began a policy of harsh repression that turned his own people against him. He was overthrown and killed in a military coup on November 2, 1963.

Since then, while the war with the Communist guerrillas (known as the Vietcong) has intensified, there has been a succession of government coups. Obviously, no permanent system of government can develop in South Vietnam until the struggle with the Hanoi regime and its supporters in the South is resolved.

Laos, although a Buddhist monarchy, has in recent years had a progression of events similar to Vietnam's because, like Vietnam, it has been the victim of large-scale Communist aggression. Ruled loosely by the French before World War II, Laos was declared independent by its Japanese occupiers prior to their defeat. When the French returned, they reinstated colonial domination. But as the French Vietminh struggle developed in Vietnam, the Vietminh invaded Laos and the French gradually diminished their control. In October, 1953, France recognized Laos as fully independent.

Under the 1954 Geneva agreement the Communists were to halt acts of aggression and subversion in Laos. A parliamentary democracy was established with the king as titular head of state, and for a time the Pathet Lao participated in a coalition government. The Pathet Lao (Laos Fatherland) is the name of a Communist-directed front organization. This coalition broke up in renewed fighting between the anti-Communists and the Pathet Lao, which was aided by Communist North Vietnamese forces. At one stage a neutralist coup led by youthful Captain Kong Le temporarily toppled the government in Vientiane, the administrative capital of Laos. An international conference held in Geneva in 1961 brought about the 1962 agreement to end the fighting in Laos on the basis of a coalition of the neutralists, the Pathet Lao and the anti-Communists. The factions clashed when it came to carrying out the agreement, and occasional fighting among them has since occurred.

Nearing the end of 1965, more than half of Laos is under a Communist-led Pathet Lao regime backed by North Vietnam but not internationally recognized. The rest of the country is under an administration in which King Savang Vatthana is titular head of state and Prince Souvanna Phouma presides as premier over a delicate balance of military and political factions. World powers and the United Nations recognize the King's government as the legitimate government of Laos. The smallest in population of the Southeast Asian lands—with 2 million people in an area of 91,000 square miles, almost as large as Oregon—Laos has little chance of working out a permanent system of self-rule until its Communist problem is settled.

VII

Independence: A Legacy of Problems

IN THE EARLY NINETEEN-FIFTIES the Western world adopted the word "underdeveloped" to describe the independent nations that came into existence after World War II. As time went on, the word seemed to suggest a static, changeless state, and it was deemed preferable to speak of "developing" rather than "underdeveloped" countries.

Actually the new nations of Southeast Asia are both "developing" and "underdeveloped." They certainly are not static. Year by year they change enormously as they look for progress and adjust to internal and external forces. Still in their economic, social and political adolescence, these countries face numerous grave and interrelated problems on their way to maturity.

For example, the problem of what political system to adopt is closely bound up with the problem of economic development and with the problem of who is to exercise economic power.

In those Southeast Asian nations that have chosen some degree of Marxist authoritarian rule—Socialist Burma, Indonesia, Cambodia and Communist North Vietnam—leaders argue that governmental control is necessary to organize backward societies and centralize the use of resources so as to achieve rapid economic and social progress. These leaders also say that their people are not unified enough, not educated enough, not politically sophisticated enough to operate democratic governments.

In addition, the urge of some Southeast Asian leaders to have and use personal power has been a factor in the adoption of authoritarianism. General Ne Win in Burma, President Sukarno in Indonesia, Prince Norodom Sihanouk in Cambodia and the Communist leaders in North Vietnam have found dictatorial controls useful not only to achieve certain national aims but also to lengthen their own rule. They have also been attracted to a Marxist type of system because it shows them a relatively simple and clear-cut way to deal with private property and business, particularly that property and business controlled by foreigners.

At the time the Southeast Asian countries gained independence, businessmen, merchants and traders with the most money, property and influence were foreigners or of foreign origin—Chinese, Indians and Westerners. Official Marxist doctrine has made it easy for the authoritarian leaders to destroy or take over the foreign interests through such techniques as nationalization.

Conditions conducive to Marxist solutions in some Southeast Asian countries were illustrated by the situation in Burma during my visits in the early nineteen-fifties, not long after the Burmese had gained independence.

The main department store in Rangoon, the Burmese capital, was a dowdy British-owned establishment. The leading banks were British and Indian. The shop where I got my photographs developed was run by a Chinese. The only comfortable hotel, the Strand, was British-owned and managed by an Armenian. Most retailing was in the hands of Indians or Chinese. In Burma's interior the oil fields and silver, lead and tungsten mines were British-owned. Except for the officials who had taken power when independence was won, the Burmese were by and large the carriers of water and cutters of wood in their own country.

In Jakarta on Java it was the Chinese and the Dutch who controlled business; in the Indochinese countries it was the Chinese and the French; in Malaysian cities the Chinese, Indians and British; in Manila the Chinese and the Americans; in Bangkok the Chinese and Westerners of many nationalities. The large number of these minority groups in business is due to several factors. Colonial rule had given Westerners and, in some lands, the Chinese and Indians advantages over the native majority people. But it is also true that because of cultural traits Southeast Asians traditionally have not been attracted to or shown aptitude for shopkeeping, trading and finance. This left business open to the near monopoly of others with more acquisitiveness, entrepreneurial drive and acumen.

For the Marxist-minded Southeast Asian leaders, nationalization not only dispossessed the private businessmen but also gave good managerial positions, salaries and other gains to the new ruling classes. Socialism provided, for the insecure, the certainty of rigid ideologies and formulas for procedure that are not characteristic of practical liberal democracy. It also furnished the justification for individuals who had assumed political power to take over economic power as well, all in the name of nationalism and the people.

The democratic Southeast Asian countries have also trimmed, in varying degrees, the economic privileges of minority business groups. Thailand, the Philippines, Laos, South Vietnam and Malaysia all have restrictions on Chinese and Westerners in some business fields. However, having chosen mostly free-enterprise economic systems, these countries have not dispossessed minority businessmen as a general policy. The liberal democratic type of government adopted by the Philippines and Malaysia includes respect for individual and property rights and thus is opposite to nationalization.

These two democratic countries have by and large accepted the principle that free-enterprise capitalism, within the limits of state economic plans and controls, offers a better way to social and economic development than the Marxist-based systems some nations employ. And so far the record shows that the best results have been achieved in the democratic states.

Of Burma under General Ne Win, Dennis Bloodworth, a British correspondent who visited Burma in April, 1965, wrote:

> The socialization program has virtually wiped out British investments. Last month the Burma Corporation (oil) was taken over, and Burma Unilever was turned into "People's Soap Factory Number One." No compensation has been paid.
>
> Foreigners are not the only sufferers, however. General Ne Win has disbanded all types of association (unless purely religious) and abolished all political parties except his own Burma Socialist Program Party. Nearly all opposition leaders are under arrest. All important

newspapers have been closed down. Trade unions have been replaced with "People's Workers' Councils."

Trade has been nationalized; industry is almost entirely in government hands. "People's Stores Corporation" has taken over nearly all wholesale and retail distribution. All banks have long since become "people's banks."

Indonesia has not yet gone this far in the socialization program. Guy J. Pauker, a specialist on Indonesian affairs, wrote after a visit to the country in 1964 that under Indonesian Communist pressure President Sukarno's government had become "a mere form of transition toward a Communist state." Sukarno himself said, "I lead the Indonesian people and state on the basis of a people's democracy."

On April 25, 1965, President Sukarno moved a step further in Burma's direction by ruling that all foreign enterprises in Indonesia not already taken over by the government be put under government control. Obviously, actions such as this give private enterprise, both foreign and domestic, little future in Indonesia.

One motivation for socialization, as we have noted, was the extraordinary grip of Chinese settlers on Southeast Asian economies in the early independence years. These Chinese are both a major asset and a tremendous problem. The most numerous immigrant minority, they began to move into Southeast Asia on a large scale in the last century to escape the poverty, unrest and growing overpopulation of their own country.

All Southeast Asian nations now bar Chinese immigrants, but in colonial days and for a period thereafter they swarmed down from China over land and by junk and steamer. They were admitted because of their willingness to work hard in new agricultural and industrial enterprises. Many came originally as contracted laborers. Most went into business after a time and prospered, contributing enormously to the development of every Southeast Asian country.

Indonesia has almost 3 million Chinese. Thailand has some 3 million still classifiable as Chinese and several million others, born in Thailand, who now call themselves Thais. Vietnam has more than a million Chinese; Cambodia, 400,000; Burma 500,000; the Philippines, 350,000; Laos 50,000; and Malaysia, before Singapore's withdrawal, had 4.5 million, almost half its total population.

The majority of the Chinese have become citizens of the countries to which they migrated. Most of them are loyal to their new homelands, but the extent of this loyalty depends on the attitudes of the people among whom they have settled. Among tolerant people like the Thais, the Chinese have intermarried and been absorbed at a fast rate; among

Moslems like the Indonesians and Malays for whom intermarriage is forbidden by Islamic religious laws, the Chinese have mostly remained as a separate and distinct group.

The Chinese who have not accepted citizenship in Southeast Asian states and have withheld their loyalties show varying degrees of enthusiasm for either the Chinese Communist government in Peking or the Chinese Nationalist government on Taiwan. This fact causes conflicts between their interests and those of their host countries, particularly if the Chinese are loyal to Peking. They become instruments for Communist penetration.

The Chinese in Malaysia present a special case because, despite Singapore's withdrawal, they still form a large proportion of the population. And they make Malaysia distinctive among Southeast Asian nations because, more than any other country in the area, Malaysia is partly the creation of Chinese immigrants. It is not a question in Malaysia whether or not other peoples there are willing to absorb the Chinese; instead the Chinese are so numerous that they have had to be accepted just as they are, retaining their "Chineseness" alongside the characteristic qualities of the other Malaysia social groups in a multi-language democracy.

Because of their economic dominance and their status as an immigrant rather than a native people, the Chinese in Malaysia have wisely accepted certain limitations in agreement with the other main Malaysian community, the native Moslem Malays. While retaining the right to keep their own language and religion, the Chinese recognize Malay as the Malaysian national language and Islam as the state religion. They accept as Malaysia's monarch a king elected from among the Malay sultans of Malaya and have agreed to special Malay rights in government jobs and certain occupations. Their own eligibility for citizenship is subject to restrictions that do not apply to Malays. However, in Singapore the Chinese, who make up 80 per cent of the population, are in firm control. They wield the political power and have a near monopoly of shops, factories and trade.

Along with the Chinese, many Indians flooded into Burma and what is now Malaysia in the days of the British Empire. Like the Chinese, the Indians were shrewd businessmen and made an important place for themselves. Consequently, after Burma and Malaysia gained independence the Indians were one of the disliked foreign minorities. In Burma, where they totaled a million and far outnumbered the Chinese, they have been deported by the hundreds of thousands and their businesses have been taken over. In Malaysia, where Indians today number slightly more than a million, they have been treated like the Chinese—that is, given citizenship if they want it and full rights if they are willing to recognize certain special Malay privileges.

Curiously enough, while the process of dealing with the entrenched positions of foreign minorities in Burma and Indonesia has reinforced authoritarian tendencies, in Malaysia the existence of large and varied racial and religious groups has favored democratic development. So far the different communities in Malaysia have realized that only through mutual democratic tolerance is coexistence possible; the obvious alternative would be bloody civil war and the end of the Federation of Malaysia.

In addition to ethnic groups of foreign origin like the Chinese and Indians, the Southeast Asian countries have purely native minorities that present problems. In Burma these problems have been so serious that its very existence as a nation has been endangered. The lowland Burmese—the majority people of what is technically the Union of Burma—constitute three-quarters of the population. The remainder is made up of about 3 million hill-dwelling Shans, 2 million Karens, 500,000 Kachins of the far northern mountains and less numerous Mons, Chins, Nagas and others.

These minorities have resisted domination by the Burmese ever since independence. The fact that the Burmese are Buddhists and most of the minorities are not has intensified hostilities. Minority rebellions have been a continuous drain on the government; and the "minority" problem may yet make the

Union of Burma eventually unworkable under the present structure of its government. One justification General Ne Win has put forward for his authoritarian regime is that firm central control over the minorities is necessary to prevent a breakup of the Union. When he ousted U Nu's government he moved to minimize minority opposition to the Burmese on at least one issue by dropping Nu's plan to make Buddhism the state religion. But minority revolts continue.

In all the other Southeast Asian countries ethnic or religious minorities similarly resist central control. In the Philippines it is the fierce little Moros in Mindanao and the Sulu islands to the south—a Moslem minority of 1.5 million among a predominantly Christian people—who are lawless and uncompromising. In Indonesia dissatisfied Moslem as well as Christian groups have been in rebellion in a largely Islamic state. However, the minority problem has nowhere else been as serious as in Burma.

All Southeast Asian problems would of course be easier to solve if the major difficulties of economic and social development could be surmounted. And these would be overcome in less time if governments were more effective and more concerned with the welfare of their people.

In Southeast Asian societies, where illiteracy and poverty are still endemic, governments suffer from shortages of trained personnel, money and equipment. When Indonesia gained independence, there were only a few hundred Indonesians who had attended universities. Laos had only a few score university graduates and exactly one fully qualified physician.

Other countries, somewhat better off, were still sadly short of people with both higher education and administrative experience. Government departments were lucky to possess a typewriter—to say nothing of the more complicated office machines that Western governments regard as absolutely necessary. Telephones were so few and so unreliable that officials often left their desks and traveled for an hour through city traffic to get in touch with someone they could have reached in three minutes had a phone connection been possible. Thus, these inefficient, inexperienced, poorly staffed governments plagued with corruption have been faced with problems that would daunt the world's most competent governments.

A major economic difficulty lies in the fact that Southeast Asian countries are mainly producers of agricultural products—rice, copra, rubber, sugar, timber, sisal, hemp, palm oil, tobacco, tea, fruits, etc. Some do have important minerals: tin in Malaysia, Indonesia and Thailand; iron ore in Malaysia; oil in Indonesia and Burma; coal in North Vietnam. But whether their raw materials are mineral or agricultural, they have to be sold to the advanced industrial nations at whatever prices are offered. From the payments for what they sell, the Southeast Asian countries have to buy from abroad the manufactured goods they are still unable to make for themselves. The terms of this exchange are financially unfavorable to them.

Tan Siew Sin, the shrewd little Chinese Finance Minister of Malaysia, spoke on that subject when I last saw him in Kuala Lumpur, Malaysia's capital:

> While the prices of manufactured goods continue to rise, the long-term trend in the prices of primary products [raw materials], on the whole, is either downward or stationary. This means that the developing countries have to produce an ever increasing volume of primary products in order to buy the same or sometimes even a smaller volume of manufactured goods from the industrialized countries.

Thus, like Alice in Wonderland, the Southeast Asian countries—striving for economic progress—have to run faster and faster merely to stay in the same place.

Fast-growing populations and their demands for higher standards of living have intensified the difficulties posed by unfavorable terms of trade and inadequate government funds. When the independence era began in Southeast Asia after World War II, population was a problem only in crowded Indonesia. Today the zooming rates of increase—around 3 per cent in most Southeast Asian countries—make overpopulation a problem throughout the area.

In Indonesia the population in 1965 rose to more than 104 million, of which roughly 71 million were on Java, an island about the size of Alabama. Within Singapore's 225 square miles live 2 million people who are increasing at the record pace of 4.3 per cent a year. Unless something is done to check the present rates of population growth—and little effort is being exerted by governments on the task so far—Southeast Asia could, by the end of the century, have more than twice today's 245 million people.

Population pressure aggravates the long-standing problem of land rights and agricultural output. Particularly in the Philippines, but to some degree in all Southeast Asian countries where arable areas are overcrowded and tilled in small plots by millions of peasants, there exist landlordism and inefficient production. Crop yields are below those in Taiwan and Japan, where the majority of farmers own their own land and use scientific methods of cultivation. Southeast Asian nations need both to end landlordism and to improve agricultural techniques, but in most countries the ruling classes are barriers to effective action.

All Southeast Asian countries have tried to overcome the disadvantages of their economic depend-ence on primary products by starting manufacturing industries of their own. Most now have textile plants, consumer-goods factories and enterprises that process some of their raw materials. Foreign economic aid has helped. Since the end of World War II the United States has pumped millions of dollars worth of goods and technical advice into Southeast Asian countries—with the Philippines as the biggest recipient. Britain has also been a major donor, particularly to Malaysia. In addition, Japan, France, Australia, Canada and West Germany among Free World countries have carried on aid programs of considerable size in this area.

Communist-bloc nations have competed with Western lands in assisting the neutralist Southeast Asian states and have been the sole source of foreign aid to Communist North Vietnam. At one stage neutralist Cambodia was getting a 500-bed hospital from the Soviet Union, hospital equipment from the United States, a 30,000-man army equipped and paid by the Americans but trained by the French, a radio station and various small factories from Communist China, a tractor assembly plant from Czechoslovakia, surgical instruments from Poland, money for a dam from Yugoslavia and technical help on vegetable growing from Japan. Similar aid patterns developed in Burma and Indonesia. In a swing toward the Communist bloc Prince Sihanouk of Cambodia refused further United States aid of all types in 1963; and by mid-1964 Burma and Indonesia also had become so hostile to the United States and the West that only a trickle of Western aid continued to those two nations.

In a number of Southeast Asian countries, the goods and expertise supplied by foreign aid have made the difference between some progress and very little or none at all. In not one of the new nations has there been sufficient domestic capital or technical skill to achieve unaided the "take-off" for self-sustaining economic growth. Even in the Philippines, Malaysia, Thailand and Cambodia, where foreign aid has been relatively well utilized in combination with domestic resources, self-sustaining growth is still not possible. More foreign aid will be necessary, but the prospects are hopeful. For Indonesia, Burma and war-torn Laos and Vietnam, where economic progress lags while populations swell, the outlook is grim.

The search for identity—the urge by new governments and leaders to assert themselves and attract attention at home and abroad—has been a typical characteristic of the independence era in Southeast Asia. Sukarno of Indonesia has spent hundreds of thousands of dollars on showy global tours to demonstrate his and his country's importance in the world. In Jakarta, Indonesia's capital, a vast new sports center built by the Soviet Union is kept brightly lighted at night as a symbol of national revival. In Cambodia Prince Sihanouk has lavished large sums on boulevards, parks and public buildings to make Pnompenh, his capital, a showplace.

Expenditures such as these may possibly boost national morale, but they also drain off resources from social and economic development. Likewise, the continued attacks against a colonialism that no longer exists hamper cooperation with the West and lessen the benefits that could be gained from such cooperation.

VIII

Communist Aggression: The Background

WORLD WAR II started the countries of Southeast Asia on the road to independence. Born out of turmoil, they have experienced conflict ever since. Internal quarrels have accounted for some of the strife, and disagreements between states for some; but the main source of violence and disruption has been the struggle for and against Communism, intensified and complicated by the participation of powers from outside Southeast Asia.

Shortly after the Russian Revolution of 1917 Lenin's Comintern (International Communist Movement)—hitting at capitalist powers through their colonies—began the first Communist revolutionary activity in Southeast Asia. By 1920 Dutch Communists had organized Asia's first Communist Party in Indonesia (then the Dutch East Indies). By 1925 Red agents had Communist groups operating in every Southeast Asian land.

One of the earliest Comintern agents in Southeast Asia was Ho Chi Minh. Of all the adventurous leaders of early Southeast Asian Communism, only Ho survives. As President of the tough little Communist state of North Vietnam, he is the famed living symbol of the forces that United States troops are fighting today.

In France in the early nineteen-twenties Ho helped organize the French Communist Party. Later he slipped in and out of Indochina, China, Thailand and Hong Kong, organizing Communist movements. In 1930 he formed the Indochina Communist Party—and today he is still its leader. Ho's and other Communist parties in Southeast Asia staged strikes, mass demonstrations and small uprisings in their efforts to bring Communism to power. But they overreached themselves. Efficient colonial police searched out and arrested the parties' leaders and shattered their organizations. By 1933 the parties had been reduced to ineffectiveness. Ho himself was caught by the British in Hong Kong in 1931 and jailed for two years.

The Pacific phase of World War II presented the Communists with the opportunity to rebuild their influence. Taking an anti-Japanese position, Communist movements with guerrilla resistance bands won support from the masses, who resented Japanese domination. They also won support in varying degrees from the Allies fighting the Japanese. With possession of both guns and a strengthened political position at war's end, Communists in Southeast Asia —like their brethren in the Soviet Union and China —took the view that Southeast Asia's colonial regimes should be replaced by Communism in keeping with Marxist-Leninist doctrines.

Yet they saw colonialism hanging on in certain countries and yielding in others to independent governments that were nationalist rather than Communist. The Communist struggle against these developments during the immediate postwar years set Southeast Asia on fire with revolutionary warfare. In some countries this warfare has subsided; in some it still goes on 20 years later. In Vietnam it not only continues but has involved the United States in one of the most brutal and bitter conflicts of modern times.

When the British let Ho Chi Minh out of jail in 1933, he slipped into China. In an article in *The New York Times Magazine* in 1954 my wife sketched his activities during and just after World War II:

By 1941 there were many nationalist émigré Vietnamese organizations in South China; Ho brought them together to form a united front against French-Japanese fascism. This new body was called Vietnam Doc Lap Dong Minh Hoi—Vietminh for short. Its aim was the creation of an independent Vietnamese republic; a small hard core of Communists controlled the new organization. Under Ho, its general secretary, the Vietminh built secret cells in Japanese-controlled Vietnam.

Arrested on orders of the Nationalist government in Chungking (China's wartime capital), Ho, alias Nguyen Ai Quoc, sent word from prison in Luichow to southern General Chiang Fa-kwei that he could, if released, organize an intelligence network for China and her allies in northern Vietnam. General Chiang realized it was no use asking Generalissimo Chiang Kai-shek for permission to let Vietnamese Communist Nguyen Ai Quoc out of jail. The matter was solved by Ho's once more changing his alias. Nguyen Ai Quoc became Ho Chi Minh—"He Who Shines." Chungking authorized his release and paid a monthly sum to maintain his espionage system.

Through the remainder of the war, Ho trained Vietminh cadres [leaders of core groups] and guerrillas in South China, extended Vietminh cells in Indochina, and sent Vo Nguyen Giap—who had been to Yenan and learned in that Chinese Communist center to admire Mao Tse-tung's theories of revolutionary war—to organize guerrillas in Tongking (today's North Vietnam).

In late 1944 Ho slipped secretly into northern Tongking. After the Japanese surrender he formed a provisional government for Vietnam, and on September 2, 1945, he proclaimed Vietnam independent, quoting from the American Declaration of Independence and the French Revolution Declaration of the Rights of Man. Six months later he was elected President of the Vietnamese Republic.

The anti-Communist Chungking government of China was not the only Allied agency to give help to Communist Ho Chi Minh at a crucial time. Before the end of the war with the Japanese, Americans assigned to the Office of Strategic Services (OSS) airdropped arms to Vietminh guerrillas in northern Tongking, and right after the war encouraged Ho's provisional government in Hanoi to resist the efforts of France to reestablish its authority in Vietnam. In those days Ho was saying little about Communism and talking of freedom and democracy; moreover, OSS agents thought they were correctly interpreting President Roosevelt's opposition to the resumption of French colonial rule in Indochina. Ironically, today it is the French who want the Americans to get out of Vietnam.

When the French set about dealing with Indochina after World War II, they rejected the independence Ho had declared. Unlike the British and the Americans, who emerged from the war recognizing that independence for Southeast Asian colonies was unavoidable, the French would not entertain the idea. They would have granted self-rule, equal rights with Frenchmen, free speech, even French citizenship, but not independence. In lengthy negotiations with the Vietminh, the French finally agreed to a substantial Vietnamese self-rule within the French Union which unites France and French colonial territories.

Under one French-Vietminh agreement, French troops were allowed in Hanoi and other parts of North Vietnam upon the withdrawal of the Chinese Nationalist armies that had taken over from the Japanese. But the broader negotiations finally broke down over the degree of self-government Vietnam would have and over the status of Cochin China (now South Vietnam), where the French wanted more control than in the North. When the opposed views clearly made any compromise impossible, Ho Chi Minh ordered General Vo Nguyen Giap to launch an offensive on December 19, 1946, aimed at driving the French out of Indochina. A long savage war that was to last almost eight years began.

In other Southeast Asian lands Communists continued for some time after the Vietminh uprising to maneuver for advantage in collaboration with non-Communist independence forces. Then in late 1947 high-ranking Communist councils seem to have decided the situation was ripe for outright Communist revolution all through Southeast Asia.

Significantly, this was the time when negotiations under General George C. Marshall for peace in China between the Communists and the Nationalists broke down and Mao's Communist armies began full-scale warfare against Chiang Kai-shek's Nationalists. There is strong evidence that an order from Moscow for uprisings was transmitted to Southeast Asian Communist parties in February, 1948. Within months, uprisings flared where Communists commanded the means to revolt.

Taking advantage of the misery of tenant farmers, corruption in government and popular resentment of the glaring wealth of a small upper class, the Communists in the Philippines swept over much of the countryside of Luzon, the nation's largest and most important island. By mid-1950 they threatened to capture Manila. Luckily, the government was able to discover and arrest a group of top Communist leaders who had papers disclosing their campaign plans. In addition, Ramon Magsaysay appeared as defense minister and later as president to push the anti-Communist drive and relieve the causes of popular discontent. The tide turned. By

1953 Communist power was broken in the Philippines.

The Communists lost in the Philippines because in an already independent country they did not have the issue of nationalism to exploit. And a popular reformer in the person of Magsaysay, helped by extensive United States aid, rallied the people against the Communists.

The course of events was similar in Malaya before it became part of Malaysia. There, beginning in June, 1948, some 10,000 to 12,000 men—mostly Chinese operating in small bands—attacked plantations, mines, highway traffic and police posts from jungle hideouts. For years they caused widespread disruptions and thousands of deaths.

As the British hurried Malaya toward independence, resettled Chinese rural supporters of the rebels in guarded villages, developed a network of informers and intensified deep jungle patrolling, they slowly suppressed the Communist rebels. In 1960, after Malaya had become independent, "the emergency" was declared over. However, Communist bands still exist in remote parts of both the Philippines and Malaysia, waiting for a new opportunity.

Dissatisfied with the Indonesian Communist Party's leadership, Moscow sent a young Indonesian named Musso, who had been in exile in the Soviet Union, to launch the Indonesian rebellion.

The uprising of 3,000 men went off half-cocked. Troops of the new Indonesian Republic, then fighting the Dutch for independence, soon shattered the rebel forces and at Sukarno's orders executed Musso and other Communist leaders. The Musso revolution never had a chance. Outraged Indonesians regarded it as an act of treachery against the patriotic warriors locked in battle with the Netherlands.

It has taken many years, but the Indonesian Communist Party has risen spectacularly from the ashes of its 1948 defeat. In the early nineteen-fifties, under the new leadership of a shrewd young chairman, Dipa Nusantara Aidit, the Party abandoned its radical posture. It now emphasizes nationalism, reform and cooperation with progressive forces in society rather than class warfare and violent revolution. Building up a corps of well-trained active leaders and an efficient, disciplined organization, the Party has championed the interests of peasants, workers, teachers and students and has attracted a tremendous following. Above all, it has worked itself into favor with Sukarno, the man who ordered its leaders shot in 1948. This it has done by applauding his emotional nationalism, supporting his authoritarian "guided democracy" and serving his purposes as a counterbalance against that other powerful Indonesian political force, the armed services.

Today the Indonesian Communist Party claims 3

million regular members and 17 million other followers in front organizations that include workers,
peasants, students and teachers. The Party is the
most powerful single political force in Indonesia; its
influence has grown so strong that today it can frequently bend Sukarno to its will rather than merely
collaborate with him. Through Sukarno the Party
has prevented even his close non-Communist followers from organizing against it, and it is able to
bar the appointment or reduce the powers of officials it regards as hostile. It provides many of the
ideas and programs of the government. Chief opposition to the Communists has long rested with the
armed services, but the Communists have extensively penetrated them.

In August, 1965, *New York Times* correspondent
Seymour Topping wrote after a visit to Indonesia:
"Nearing the end of his career, President Sukarno
has decided to use the Indonesian Communist Party
as the instrument for establishing his socialist state.
He has found the Communists have the discipline,
techniques of mass organization and corruption-free
leadership needed to build his greater Indonesia.
Ruthlessly, in the last months, he has cut down the
men—even such revolutionary heroes in the government as Deputy Premier Chaerul Saleh—who have
tried to stem the push of the Communists toward
power."

Aidit says the Communist Party can come to

power without armed revolution. However, he continues to try to acquire a military capability, the lack of which is now his greatest weakness. He has urged Sukarno to permit the Communists to organize armed guerrillas for such purposes as fighting the Dutch when they held West Irian, and more lately for combat in Malaysia. But with the army firmly opposed, Sukarno has rebuffed these pleas.

Though strong on the key island of Java, the Communists are weak on the other islands. They hardly seem powerful enough to attempt to take over Indonesia when Sukarno dies, but they could well be the directing force behind some front man or group. Indonesian Chinese provide much of the Party's finances, and the Party has taken a pro-Peking line in the Soviet-Chinese dispute without, however, quarreling completely with the Russians.

When the Burmese Communist Party went into revolt in 1948 against the government of Burma, it had considerable initial success. But it soon lost momentum. It lacked a basis for appeal against a newly independent regime in a country with a regular rice surplus and no sharp peasant dissatisfactions, at least among the people making up the majority of the population. But the Party manages to continue fighting from jungle hideouts. At present no major threat, Burma's Communists could become one any time the Chinese Communists choose to give them more guns and backing.

In Thailand, where the Communists were weak, only minor outbreaks have occurred since 1948. However, a Communist organization—linked to Peking and Communist Thai exiles in China—has secretly remained in existence. In the early nineteen-sixties, an underground Communist movement became active among the peasants in the poverty-stricken area next to Laos. Obviously a carry-over from Communism in Laos, Communist China and North Vietnam, the activity in Thailand leads back to the situation that grew out of General Giap's 1946 offensive against the French.

IX

Communist Aggression: The First Vietnam War

THE VIETMINH offensive against the French started with an outburst of sabotage, assassinations and guerrilla raids in the usual style of Communist warfare in its initial stages. Before the campaign was over, almost eight years later, massive forces were engaged in combat on both sides—for the Vietminh 200,000 regulars, 150,000 organized guerrillas and hundreds of thousands of irregular partisans; for the French a foreign expeditionary corps of 190,000 men plus cooperating Vietnamese, Laotian and Cambodian regulars and auxiliaries totaling 225,-000. General Giap succeeded in his aim. He defeated the French, and a century of French rule in Indochina was brought to an end.

Thus, Ho Chi Minh's Vietminh became the only

Communist movement in Southeast Asia to triumph decisively in the revolutionary wave that swept the region after World War II. This success was, however, part of Communism's general advance in Asia. Ho's victory would have been impossible without Communist success in China and the guns, food and training facilities the Chinese Communists gave the Vietminh in the later stages of their struggle against the French.

The French also received massive outside aid. This came from the United States in the form of military equipment, economic assistance and political support. In the last months of the war the United States would have joined the fighting with air support if the British had not refused to do likewise. United States help also extended to recognizing and trying to increase the prestige of the French-sponsored Bao Dai government in Vietnam and the royal regimes of Laos and Cambodia.

But the French could not overcome the disastrous effects of their military and political mistakes. They would not give the government of Bao Dai, the former emperor of the prewar state of Annam in Central Vietnam, enough independence to enable it to attract popular support. French forces proved unable to cope with the Vietminh's guerrilla tactics and its techniques for organizing and controlling the population. And they capped their many mistakes by making a defense fortress out of Dienbienphu—a town, rimmed by hills deep in Vietminh territory, that could be supplied only by air from Hanoi, 180 miles away. General Giap surrounded it and blasted it with artillery the French had thought he could never transport over mountain trails from China. The Vietminh overran the stronghold on May 7, 1954, after a bloody siege.

The chief function of the Geneva Conference of 1954—attended by the United States, Britain, France, the Soviet Union, Communist China, North and South Korea, Laos, Cambodia, the Bao Dai and Vietminh governments of Vietnam and other parties —was to negotiate an end to the Indochina fighting. The Conference agreements left the Vietminh with the northern half of Vietnam, from the 17th Parallel. Through their Laotian collaborators the Vietminh also retained a territorial stake in northern Laos. The southern half of Vietnam went to the Bao Dai regime.

Having established a clear military superiority over the French, the Vietnamese Communists were disappointed at what they got from the Geneva Conference. One reason they accepted the Geneva decisions was pressure from the Soviet Union and Communist China. Both feared that a prolongation of the war would bring the armed forces of the United States into combat on the side of France.

The fact that the future looked very favorable to them was an element making the Geneva agreements somewhat more acceptable to the Vietnamese Communists. The governments of South Vietnam, Laos and Cambodia were weak. They would be weaker still when the large French military force withdrew from Indochina in accordance with the Geneva agreements. Vietnamese Communist goals remained what they had originally been when Ho Chi Minh organized a Communist party for all Indochina, not just Vietnam. Consequently, the Vietnamese Communists signed the Geneva agreements with the firm intention of renewing, at an opportune time, their drive to the south. They felt confident of their ability to overcome and destroy any non-Communist governments that stood in their way.

During the war against the French the Vietminh had enormously widened its influence in Laos. Laotians who had worked with the Vietminh in North Vietnam occupied parts of northern and eastern Laos with supporting Vietminh troops. The Laotian Communists now operate through a Communist-directed front organization, the Pathet Lao. Prince Souphanouvong of Laos is the official head of the Pathet Lao.

The Vietminh found it harder to build a Communist movement in Cambodia than in Laos. Communist guerrillas were active in Cambodia during the conflict with the French, but they were mostly Vietnamese who were living in that country. No full-blooded Cambodian emerged as a Communist leader. However, a Communist Party has developed under North Vietnamese sponsorship and has gained enough influence, especially among young Cambodian intellectuals, to cause Prince Sihanouk real concern. In 1962 he had fourteen Party members arrested; the government found documents clearly indicating not only North Vietnamese direction of Cambodian Communists but also plans to gain control of the army, the teachers and the Buddhist clergy.

To keep its hands free and avoid formal approval of a Communist conquest, the United States did not sign the Geneva agreements. After they were concluded, it stepped boldly in with support programs for South Vietnam, Cambodia and Laos, hoping to strengthen those states so that they would be able to withstand Communist attempts to expand. Knowledgeable Americans knew that the risks of United States involvement in renewed strife and vast political entanglements were great; events have lived up to their worst expectations.

In almost no time at all after the Geneva accords were signed on July 21, 1954, a flare-up of violence in South Vietnam gave an indication of the trials that were to come.

At Geneva the French at long last had signed an agreement giving Vietnam full independence; and during the conference Bao Dai, South Vietnam's chief of state, appointed Ngo Dinh Diem as South Vietnam's premier. The Americans had wanted Diem named because he had remained aloof from the South Vietnamese government during the war and was therefore untainted by collaboration with French colonialism. He also seemed to be a patriotic anti-Communist Vietnamese of high principle. But both the French and Bao Dai disliked him because of his independent attitude. They grudgingly accepted his taking the office, and then promptly began to plot against him.

Although the French were on their way out as rulers in Indochina, they planned to keep wide economic and political influence there. Their defeat by the Vietminh had convinced them that the future of Vietnam and possibly of all Indochina lay with the Communists, and they regarded the Geneva agreements as only a makeshift transition to Communist rule of all Vietnam. They did not think any Vietnamese government in the South could withstand the power and influence of the North, and they based their policy on the belief that they could get along with the Communists. Therefore, France sent a mission to Hanoi under Ho Chi Minh's old admirer Jean Sainteny and plotted to get the firmly anti-Communist Diem out of power in Saigon. They hoped to see control there come into the hands of a pro-French group of compromisers who would come to terms with the new Democratic Republic of

North Vietnam.

Thus, Diem took over in Saigon in an atmosphere of hostility. Encouraged by Bao Dai and the French, armed forces of the gangster-like Binh Xuyen organization and the Cao Dai and Hoa Hao religious sects revolted. Diem met the challenge head on. He knew compromise would mean a government of corrupt, quarreling factions that would have no chance of survival against the Communists. A short, stocky, stubborn Roman Catholic who felt he had a mission to save his country from Communism, Diem chose to fight rather than be displaced.

Young officers, sparked by a big jovial general named Duong Van Minh, saw Diem as a true patriot and stood by him against the remaining colonialist groups who sought to oust him. The issue came to a head when the Binh Xuyen, entrenched in the southern part of Saigon with their French advisers, started lobbing artillery shells at Diem's palace. Diem sent his young army into attack and refused demands from General Ely, the French High Commissioner, that he cease fire and negotiate.

I watched from behind telephone poles and fences just back of the tanks and infantrymen the night loyal South Vietnamese Army regulars advanced along Boulevard Gallieni, through splattering machine-gun and mortar fire, against rebel positions. The next morning I learned that General Ely's efforts to protect Diem's enemies had gone as far as a midnight telephone call to the United States Embassy. The Ambassador, General Lawton Collins, was away for consultations in Washington. In his absence a youthful chargé d'affaires, Randolph Kidder, took Ely's call and flatly refused his demand that Kidder tell Diem to order his troops to stop attacking.

In a few months Diem had cleaned up his opponents. Their leaders were killed or they fled into exile in France. Diem removed Bao Dai through a rigged referendum approving Bao Dai's dismissal and abolishing South Vietnam's quasi-monarchial status. He then declared South Vietnam a republic and was elected its first president under a new constitution.

The French got no thanks from Hanoi for their efforts in Saigon. The Sainteny mission was treated rudely. Despite this initial reverse, however, the French have never ceased to work against United States policy in Vietnam. Paris appears to believe that if the Communists take over the whole country they will stabilize it, make it independent of Moscow and Peking along the lines of Marshal Tito's Yugoslavia, and turn to France for aid and trade.

For several years after Diem consolidated his power, his regime's performance, on balance, was good. With large-scale American assistance a million refugees from the North—mostly Roman Catholics—were settled in flourishing communities in the

South. The economy, with United States aid, began
to expand; there were tranquillity, law and order,
and a rising standard of living. An American military advisory group, enlarged at the departure of a
French military training mission, made good progress in helping build a more effective army.

But by 1958 defects in the Diem regime and in
the president himself had become glaringly evident.
Increasingly the government had become a monopoly of Diem's Roman Catholic family and their
"palace favorites." Diem's chief political counselor
was a younger brother, Ngo Dinh Nhu, a warped
and devious intriguer who built up a secret party,
the Can Lao, to promote family power and control.
Nhu's wife, who lived with her husband at Diem's
palace and acted as the president's hostess, used her
position to build up her own personal following.

Another brother, Ngo Dinh Can, enforced tyrannical rule over the northern part of South Vietnam.
A third brother, Ngo Dinh Thus, a Roman Catholic
archbishop, attempted to spread the regime's influence through religious and intellectual channels. A
fourth brother, Ngo Dinh Luyen, manipulated foreign relations, most of the time as Ambassador to
Britain.

Diem himself, aloof and autocratic by tempera-
ment and training, became increasingly dictatorial,
suspicious and sensitive to criticism. He relied more
and more on a small inner circle of intimates, had

less and less contact with the people, and filled concentration camps with his critics and opponents. Like his younger brother Nhu, he became a compulsive talker. On my visits to him at this stage I was struck by the disintegration of his personality. The interviews he granted me were increasingly long monologues. I had no opportunity to ask a question or make a remark as he droned away for hours, explaining and justifying government actions and blaming others for anything that had gone wrong.

As discontent with Diem mounted, occasional outbreaks against the regime began in the countryside. Toward the end of 1957 remnants of the dissenting armies that Diem had defeated in 1954 and 1955 dug up their buried arms and started attacking government posts. Other malcontents joined in; so did the Communists. At first the Vietcong (South Vietnamese Communists) identified themselves with the Cao Dai and Hoa Hao bands, but soon they were in control and growing on their own as professed "liberation" fighters.

There is a school of thought that emphasizes the spontaneous local character of the initial outbreaks against the Diem regime and argues that the large-scale anti-government movement which eventually developed was mainly a popular uprising against tyrannical rule, an uprising aided by North Vietnam. My own conviction is that there were indeed spontaneous flare-ups against Diem, which persuaded

Communist leaders that the time was ripe to resume the Communist revolution's advance. As a result, Hanoi decided on an all-out campaign to undermine and overthrow the Diem regime and establish control in all Vietnam. From 1958 on, the mounting anti-government violence in the South has been a North Vietnam-directed Communist operation, although it has continued to embrace considerable participation by discontented non-Communists, just as the Vietminh offensive did in the war against the French.

The International Control Commission in Vietnam, established to supervise execution of the Geneva agreements, has said in a special report that there is "sufficient evidence to show beyond reasonable doubt that North Vietnam had sent arms and men into South Vietnam to carry out subversion with the aim of overthrowing the legal government there." The Canadian and Indian members of the commission signed the report; the Communist Polish member did not.

Developments in Laos may have also contributed to Hanoi's action in South Vietnam. In 1958 North Vietnam's satellite Communist front, the Pathet Lao, dropped a short-lived attempt to operate as part of the Laotian government and returned to rebellion. The need to resume violent revolution in Laos may well have decided the Vietnamese Communists to adopt the same course for South Vietnam.

Supported by North Vietnamese troops, airborne Soviet supplies and some Chinese Communist aid, the Pathet Lao threat to take over Laos and menace Thailand eventually produced a world crisis. Twice in the early nineteen-sixties the United States flew troops to Thailand to counter the Communist danger. But neither the Communist bloc nor the Western allies, when confronted with the prospect, wanted to go to war over backward, landlocked, almost roadless Laos.

Agreement was reached at another Geneva conference, this one in 1962, to neutralize the kingdom of Laos. The agreement has been widely broken, but under it the United States reduced its involvement in Laos by withdrawing its 1,600-man military mission there. Out of the Laos fighting the Vietnamese Communists secured a Pathet Lao-controlled supply route from North Vietnam through mountainous eastern Laos to South Vietnam—the famous so-called Ho Chi Minh trail. With this gain they let their Laos campaign diminish in 1964 and 1965 to concentrate on the crucial Vietnam front.

X

Communist Aggression: The Second Vietnam War

THE 1954 GENEVA AGREEMENTS, which divided Vietnam into two parts, specified that the Communists withdraw all their agents and military personnel from the South. This they did not do. Instead thousands of Communist guerrillas and political workers buried their weapons during 1954 and 1955 and melted quietly into the general population. Those Communists from the South who did go to the North were put through training courses there to prepare them for a return to the South to resume revolutionary activity.

Another provision of the Geneva agreements was that nationwide elections be held in 1956 to unify Vietnam. Like the United States, the Diem government had not signed the Geneva agreements. It re-

fused to go through with the elections, arguing that
free voting in the tightly controlled Communist
North would be impossible. The North was too busy
in 1956 with peasant riots against collective farming
to raise much of an outcry about not having elections.

Beginning with raids on rubber estates and the
murder of village officials, a second Vietnam war
developed rapidly in the South as more and more
Vietcong guerrilla bands got organized. By mid-
1959 murders of officials averaged one a day, and
by March, 1961, the average was many times that
number. Ambushes, terrorist killings in villages and
the sabotaging of roads, railways and bridges spread
throughout the South. By 1962 it was estimated that
30,000 guerrillas were active.

The United States responded to this campaign by
increasing its military advisory staff in South Vietnam from a few hundred to thousands of men, and
by stepping up its economic and technical aid in all
fields. In 1964 General Maxwell D. Taylor was
shifted from his Washington post as Chairman of
the Joint Chiefs of Staff to head for a time the expanded American effort as Ambassador in Saigon.

As the Vietcong began to get more arms and ad-
ditional manpower from the North, they became increasingly effective in dominating rural areas. They
got the support of peasants by terrorizing them, by
capitalizing on the failings of the Diem government,

by denouncing that regime's reliance on "American imperialism," by abolishing government taxes and by promising tenant farmers ownership of the land they were plowing. Such acts as disemboweling the wife of a village official and slaughtering his children before cutting the official's throat in public were effective in getting cooperation.

The reaction of the Diem regime to this enlarged threat was greater rigidity and repression. Increasingly fearful of revolt against him—several attempts between 1960 and 1963 to overthrow him having failed—President Diem distrusted all but a few favorite officials and generals. Only under heavy guard did he leave his palace, and he was forced into relying on flatterers and opportunists while able, independent-minded army officers and civil administrators were constantly shifted about to prevent conspiracies or were kept under close watch in Saigon.

In an effort to break the Vietcong's grip on the countryside, the government herded scattered peasant households into strategic clusters that were supposed to be protected and provided with welfare facilities. Poorly carried out, the program resulted in gross mistreatment of the peasants, increasing their resentment against the Diem regime.

All too clearly, the majority of the South Vietnamese people and most of the armed forces were turning against Diem. In an attempt to bring about his overthrow, his opponents worked up an anti-government movement among the country's Buddhists, making use of the preference that the Diem regime showed to Roman Catholics in making civil and military appointments and in distributing various benefits. A number of Buddhist monks drenched themselves with gasoline and burned themselves to death in public protests against the government. Diem and his brothers refused to meet Buddhist demands, and the police killed several Buddhist demonstrators and smashed up Saigon's Buddhist headquarters.

Convinced that Diem had lost so much public support that he could not possibly win the war against the Vietcong, American officials made statements disassociating the United States from his government. To underline the statements, Washington began canceling certain United States aid payments. As it became clear that neither pressure from his own people nor pressure from Washington would persuade Diem to resign, it also became obvious to the Vietnamese that the United States would approve his overthrow.

In these circumstances a group of generals decided to act. Ironically, their leader was Duong Van Minh, who had helped Diem defeat his political enemies in 1955. On November 2, 1963, they captured Diem and his brother Nhu in Saigon and had them murdered. Another brother, Can, was seized in Hue and later executed. The outcome shocked the United States government, which had hoped the overthrow could be accomplished without violence and that Diem and his family would suffer nothing worse than exile.

The South Vietnamese regime became somewhat less oppressive after the overthrow of Diem, but was no more effective. Members of the ruling tribunal quarreled with each other, General Minh was shunted aside, and eventually General Nguyen Khanh emerged as the dominant military personality. He headed the government for a period but, after a series of coups and attempted coups, was forced out by his colleagues. Phan Huy Quat, an astute and competent civilian who had been foreign minister, took over as premier with the backing of a military group in early 1965. His government showed prospects of becoming the best regime since the constructive early years of Diem's rule, but this civilian government did not last long. The military took over again in June, 1965, with air-force commander Nguyen Cao Ky as premier.

The instability after Diem's overthrow, with generals preoccupied with internal political battles rather than military affairs, contributed to further progress by the Vietcong. Moreover, the successive Saigon governments failed to rally the people's support against the Vietcong or to develop any more successful tactics for defeating them than had the

Diem regime.

As the war situation worsened, efforts to avert a Communist victory led to deeper and deeper United States involvements in Vietnam. United States military personnel—who in 1961 and 1962 were merely accompanying South Vietnamese units into combat, rarely shooting or getting shot at—were regularly shooting and getting killed or wounded by 1964. American planes and helicopters gradually began to take more and more direct action against the Vietcong. By late 1965 the number of U.S. troops in Vietnam had reached about 150,000; the United States was spending hundreds of millions of dollars a year on the Vietnam war and supporting an ever bigger South Vietnamese military force.

In August, 1964, North Vietnamese torpedo boats attacked two United States destroyers in the Gulf of Tonkin and, in retaliation, fighter-bombers took off from United States aircraft carriers to make the first American air strikes in North Vietnam. In early 1965 United States planes began bombing Vietcong supply routes in Laos. On February 8, 1965, *New York Times* correspondents in Vietnam described how during the previous night Vietcong troops had crept through the barbed wire surrounding a camp at Pleiku in the highlands of South Vietnam and shot up the American garrison of 400 as Vietcong mortars from 1,000 yards away blasted the barracks. Seven Americans were killed. President Johnson himself ordered a retaliatory air attack against North Vietnam. When 21 Americans were killed a few days later as the Vietcong blasted military quarters at the coastal city of Quinhon, a still bigger American air strike was made in the North.

By the first week of March, 1965, President Johnson and his advisers had declared that simply retaliatory air raids on the North were not enough. The United States began systematically to bomb and strafe military centers, roads, railways, bridges, radar installations and other military targets in North Vietnam. To protect the main air base for these attacks, Danang, on the northeast coast of South Vietnam, 14,000 United States Marines were landed in April and May, 1965, and were soon engaged in clashes with nearby Vietcong troops. United States Army paratroopers totaling 3,500 joined them in Vietnam in May.

By July, 1965, 503 Americans had died and more than 2,700 had been wounded. Casualties among the Vietnamese fighters on both sides totaled more than 175,000. Washington announced plans to increase South Vietnam's troops to 600,000. They would confront about 50,000 Vietcong regulars backed by 100,000 local guerrillas and a vast network of spies, propagandists and saboteurs. An army of 450,000 stood ready in North Vietnam; one of its divisions entered South Vietnam in 1965.

Communist China had supplied large quantities of new weapons to the Vietcong, and in early 1965 the Soviet Union began the work of installing anti-aircraft missiles around Hanoi in North Vietnam. These had shot down several American planes by late 1965. A battalion of Australian troops and an artillery unit from New Zealand joined in the combat on the South Vietnam side in 1965, and a division of troops from South Korea had been promised for allied forces. Flying from Guam, huge American B-52 bombers by late 1965 had begun almost daily pounding of Vietcong concentration areas in South Vietnam.

Clearly, the war had become a large-scale one. In a speech at Johns Hopkins University in April, 1965, President Johnson said the United States wanted peace and was ready for unconditional discussions with North Vietnam. He announced that the United States was ready to provide a billion dollars for Southeast Asian development in which North Vietnam could share if peace were established. At the same time, he insisted that North Vietnam must stop trying to destroy the South Vietnamese government. He emphasized United States determination to do whatever was necessary to prevent a Communist take-over in South Vietnam.

With the Vietcong in control of half of South Vietnam's 15.5 million people and more than half of the countryside in early 1965, the prospect of defeating the Communist drive by counteraction in the South alone seemed very doubtful. One objective of the United States bombing attacks on North Vietnam that began at that time was to try to force Hanoi to negotiate an acceptable settlement of the hostilities. By "acceptable" the United States meant a situation in which North Vietnam and South Vietnam would not interfere in each other's affairs. Another United States objective in attacking the North was to warn Communist China and the Soviet Union, through Washington's display of determination, against intervening in the Vietnam war.

The United States air strikes were a new departure in the fight against subversion and guerrilla action. The South Vietnamese and Americans were obviously not succeeding in their efforts to defeat Vietcong tactics on the ground in South Vietnam. By bombing North Vietnam, the United States had struck at the sanctuary that supported the guerrillas. Up to that time such sanctuaries around the world had never been attacked.

The Vietcong fight in the South is being waged ostensibly by the National Front for the Liberation of Vietnam. This organization, with headquarters in the jungles near the Cambodian border northwest of Saigon, is supposed to represent broad sections of the South Vietnamese people. There is plenty of evidence that it does contain non-Communist elements and also plenty of evidence that it is Communist-run. The South Vietnam People's Revolutionary Party (the Communist party for the South) has also been organized. With headquarters in Hanoi, the party is openly the directing force in the Liberation Front.

North Vietnam, Communist China and the Soviet Union all rejected President Johnson's offer in April, 1965, for unconditional negotiations and demanded that the United States first withdraw from South Vietnam. Moreover, Peking and Moscow made threats about intervening in the war on Hanoi's side. The Soviet Union, however, indicated a willingness to take part with other nations in a general conference on Vietnam, but has not taken any initial steps to organize such a conference.

During 1965 U.S. officials many times reiterated Washington's readiness to negotiate with North Vietnam unconditionally to end the Vietnam war, even conceding that South Vietnam rebel Liberation Front delegates would be acceptable in a Hanoi delegation. For a final settlement U.S. spokesmen have insisted that South Vietnam must be left free by the Communists to choose its own future course in accord with the Geneva agreements of 1954. They have stated that U.S. forces could be withdrawn if the North Vietnam Communists likewise withdrew their forces from South Vietnam and ceased interfering in that state's political affairs. North Vietnam has regularly rejected U.S. overtures and said a settlement could only be on a basis of U.S. withdrawal from South Vietnam. Communist China has taken a similar stand, rejecting any United Nations role in a settlement of the Vietnam war and depicting the Vietnam struggle as a part of a Peking-directed world movement of encirclement and destruction of the United States by revolutionary forces.

By September, 1965, the war was going better for South Vietnam. The monsoon offensive of the Vietcong had failed, and U.S. and South Vietnamese forces were having increasing success. The terrible destruction in the countryside by the warring forces had caused half a million South Vietnamese to leave their homes and become refugees in various safe zones. This burdened the Saigon government and the U.S., but their combat prospects were nevertheless improved.

So the struggle went on, savagely and ruthlessly. Hardly a road in South Vietnam was safe from the constant Vietcong ambushes. Across trails the Communist guerrillas dug disguised pits with sharpened bamboo spikes in the bottom to torture the unguarded. They fought in villages from networks of underground tunnels. And they killed people pitilessly to enforce cooperation and obedience among the population.

On March 30, 1965, a dispatch in *The New York Times* reported that a Vietcong bomb concealed in an automobile had shattered the U.S. Embassy in

Saigon, killing two Americans and 15 Vietnamese. And on the anti-Communist side flame-throwing tanks, mines and shrapnel plus high-explosive and burning napalm bombs dropped in Vietcong areas by American and South Vietnamese planes likewise took a bloody toll of both civilians and combatants.

Then in May, 1965, the Vietcong attacked Songbe, a South Vietnamese provincial capital, and occupied it for several hours before being driven off. A dispatch from Songbe by Jack Langguth of *The Times* made vividly clear what the war has been like for the American G.I., the South Vietnamese civilian and the Communist guerrilla embroiled in it. Here is most of that dispatch:

S. Sgt. Horace E. Young was lying wounded in the mess hall at 3 A.M. yesterday when a grenade rolled through the door.

He had been struck in the leg an hour earlier by fragments from the mortar rounds the Vietcong had used before overrunning this provincial capital.

He could hardly move. But, as the incident was related later, he tried to shove the grenade outside with the barrel of his empty rifle. The grenade exploded and ripped into his arm.

In the darkness Young, in unbearable pain, grabbed at a silhouette. "It's a friend," whispered Specialist 4 Gige E. Kelso of Alton, Ill.

"Let's try to get us a weapon," Young said.

Kelso wiped Young's blood off his face and neck.

Young pulled out a short knife and dragged himself through the mess hall, which had become a temporary aid station.

In the storeroom he struggled weakly with a youthful Vietcong who had broken into the small mess building.

Then Sergeant Young, 34 years old, of Moline, Ill., collapsed amid cans of tomato juice and bled to death.

His body was shipped to Saigon yesterday with the knife in his hand. No one had been able to pry it loose.

A PRIEST AND HIS CHURCH

The Rev. Dominic Roanh was three feet below ground yesterday morning in a covered tunnel he prepared last month.

The Communist soldiers had swarmed around his Roman Catholic church, around the central market and the town hospital, to make it harder for South Vietnamese aircraft to come after them.

Sometimes the priest's 14-year-old altar boy would slip out of the tunnel to hear what the Vietcong were saying.

From the stifling hole Father Roanh could

hear the dozens of air strikes that finally drove the Communists out of the trenches they had dug around the town.

When the priest was finally able to come out of the darkness, he found the roof of his church pounded to the earth. "I think now I have not enough money to repair it," he said.

A GUERRILLA DIES

His name may have been Le Minh Ngoc. That name, along with several aliases, was on a piece of paper found today when 1,500 government troops moved through the Songbe area looking for the withdrawing Vietcong.

Early yesterday the odds had favored Ngoc. At least 900 fellow Vietcong had attacked. . . .

The man at his left shone a flashlight into the American mess, and they looked at the liquor bottles around the bar. Their own refreshment came from hollowed bamboo stalks filled with coconut milk.

Moving through the darkness, the two Vietcong did not see Gige Kelso, crouched unarmed across the room.

One of the Vietcong came across Lieut. Col. Afton Park, the post commander, who had been hit in the first barrage. Perhaps the guerrilla shot him again through the lungs. There was confusion today about that. But Colonel Park survived.

At the storeroom Ngoc apparently heard a noise. He went in and was knifed by a dying American Special Forces sergeant.

Then the young guerrilla, wearing only shorts, pulled himself out of the mess hall. He was hit by a blast of bullets. For 30 hours his half-naked body lay in a ditch by the mess-hall door.

By noon today the Americans had finished tending to their 5 dead and 13 wounded and to the more than 40 Vietnamese government dead. Then they began to deal with the 59 Vietcong bodies.

In March, 1965, C. L. Sulzberger, *New York Times* columnist, wrote from the northern South Vietnamese city of Hue:

After all this agony of fighting—mostly for reasons they do not understand and for ideologies that make no village sense—the resilient, desperate, durable little peasants of South Vietnam dream only of peace. Peace for them means no longer losing sons, food and savings to rival armies, a chance to grow and eat crops.

But dawn is not yet perceptible in this dark night. Great wills are engaged in testing each other in places as distant as Washington and

Peking, of which few Vietnamese peasants have ever heard. Meanwhile, as Thucydides wrote of an earlier and less barbarous conflict, "The strong did what they could and the weak suffered what they must."

Such is the war that resulted from Communist determination to expand and dominate in Southeast Asia. In the conflict North Vietnam's own desire to conquer is fed by Communist China's urge to push Communism south and to always do anything that might damage their most hated enemy, the United States. Beyond Vietnam and Laos the growing activity of Communist bands in northeastern Thailand has reemphasized Communist aims to continue pushing and make Thailand, a United States ally, a future area of aggressive subversion.

XI

Indonesia versus Malaysia, Plus a Look at Cambodia's Quarrels

BEFORE 1963 President Sukarno of Indonesia used to stir his people with the cry "From Sabang to Merauke." With this slogan, referring to one town at the northern tip of Sumatra and another in the southeast corner of West New Guinea, he emphasized not only the unity of Indonesia but also his government's claim to the Dutch-ruled half of New Guinea.

After Indonesia gained control of West New Guinea (now West Irian) under a United Nations decree in August, 1962, Sukarno dropped the "Sabang to Merauke" slogan. But he has found another: "Crush Malaysia."

Declaring that the creation of a federation joining Malaya, Singapore, Sarawak and Sabah in 1963 constituted a "neo-colonialist" plot to encircle Indonesia, Sukarno's government has proclaimed its intention of destroying the new Federation of Malaysia. Almost without a break it switched from a high-pitched West Irian campaign into aggression against another neighboring territory.

All this has been accompanied by an increase in nationalistic muscle-flexing. The statements coming from Jakarta, Indonesia's capital, reflect not only expansionist territorial aims but also a new Indonesian aggressiveness in world affairs. Indonesia has withdrawn from the United Nations, drawn steadily closer to the Soviet Union and Communist China, shown violent hostility toward the United States and Britain, and become a grave new threat to nearby lands.

On the wall of his office President Sukarno has a map of the 14th-century Madjapahit Empire, one of several empires that flourished during pre-Dutch times in what is now Indonesia. Scholarly research indicates that the empire exercised effective control only in Java, Bali, Madura and probably some of Sumatra, Borneo, Celebes and the Moluccas. But Indonesians like to think of Madjapahit as having had decisive influence far beyond the present bounds of Indonesia, into the Malay peninsula, all of Borneo and part of the Philippines. Thus, to Sukarno and many of his countrymen, Madjapahit has become the symbol of the vast and powerful realm they plan to make of Indonesia. Some Indonesian leaders feel that the non-Indonesian Malay peoples —the native population of most of Malaysia and the Philippines—should be under Indonesian control or at least Indonesian influence.

There are Indonesians with even bigger ideas. Australians are dismayed to learn that some Indonesians have referred to Australian-ruled East New Guinea as East Irian and to Australia as South Irian. Sukarno has renamed the Indian Ocean the Indonesian Ocean, and Indonesian maps have been printed showing the change.

Clearly, the Federation of Malaysia is a barrier to Indonesian expansionist aims. Malaysia united two weak ex-British colonies on the North Borneo coast, Sabah and Sarawak, into a union with a fairly stable and prosperous Malaya and, until recently, the island of Singapore. And the federation not only remained in the British Commonwealth but also concluded a defense pact with Britain that made British, Australian and New Zealand forces responsible for its defense. Britain's membership in the Southeast Asia Treaty Organization (SEATO) and the membership of Australia and New Zealand in the Pacific Security Pact (ANZUS) tied Malaysia's security to the power of the United States, which is a member of both groups. Britain's big Singapore base became linked with United States bases in the Philippines. Thus, Malaysia presented Indonesia with a small but relatively strong and not very friendly neighbor instead of a potential satellite. The new state also retained along Indonesia's northern fringes the continuing presence of British power and, indirectly, American power as well. This Indonesia proclaims to be neo-colonialism.

There are other reasons for Indonesia's opposition to Malaysia. Having built themselves up with large purchases of Soviet weapons, planes and warships, the Indonesian armed forces were without a mission when the Dutch surrendered and gave up West New Guinea. The armed forces faced a cut in their budget and perhaps some demobilization.

Indonesia's powerful Communist Party wanted the government to oppose Malaysia because it was a next-door example of a successful non-Communist system. It also had ties with the capitalist West. An Indonesian stand against Malaysia would serve Communist purposes by placing Indonesia in conflict with the West.

Indeed, for the whole Sukarno regime a struggle against Malaysia opened up the prospect of a new national mission that would draw the Indonesian population's attention away from internal frictions and problems. The Communists and the armed forces, usually prone to rivalry, could make common cause against Malaysia. The necessity of settling down to the difficult tasks of economic development, which had been repeatedly sidetracked, could be ignored again. The people could be given circuses instead of bread.

Thus, despite elections in Singapore and Malaya and a United Nations survey in Sarawak and Sabah —all showing heavy majorities in support of Malaysia—the Sukarno government refused to accept the new nation. Even while it was still in the planning stage Indonesia backed a revolt in the small British-protected Borneo sultanate of Brunei with the aim of taking over not only Brunei but Sabah and Sarawak as well.

Indonesia's opposition to Malaysia ruined two promising Southeast Asian efforts at cooperation. Before Malaysia was formed, Thailand, the Philippines and Malaya figured in the first effort by joining in a compact for cooperation in cultural communications and economic affairs. But as Indonesia's hostility against Malaysia developed, the Philippines lost interest in the Association for Southeast Asia and turned to the problem of Indonesia's anti-Malaysia bias.

Philippine action took the form of laying a claim to Sabah, the former British colony of North Borneo, and joining Indonesia, though less violently, in opposition to Malaysia. The Sabah claim was based on the fact that the British North Borneo Company had acquired the territory in the 19th century from the Philippine Sultan of Sulu. Britain maintained that the territory had been ceded; the Philippines argued it had only been leased.

The second effort at cooperation occurred early in 1963 when President Macapagal of the Philippines tried to promote friendship through a scheme for close alignment between Malaysia, the Philippines and Indonesia. The scheme was called Maphilindo. As Sukarno left the Manila conference at which Maphilindo was born, he hailed its prospects of success. Once back at Jakarta, however, he soon reverted to threats against Malaysia. Indonesia refused to have any relations with the new state when it came into being in September, 1963, and proclaimed a trade ban against it.

By 1964 Jakarta had begun to translate hostility into action. Guerrillas from Indonesia started to penetrate Malaysia: many were dropped from planes, some arrived in small boats and others slipped across the Sarawak border from Indonesian Borneo.

The guerrilla attacks, combined with a build-up of regular forces in Indonesian Borneo, have provoked Malaysia and its allies to a large-scale defensive effort. Britain has rushed troops, aircraft and warships to Malaysia; Australia and New Zealand have strengthened their forces in the new Federation; and Malaysia itself has taken steps to increase its armed strength. By mid-1965 powerful British, Australian and New Zealand army, navy and airforce units with a strength of roughly 50,000 men had massed against the threat of a major attack by Indonesia, which possesses a large army, an air force of late-model Soviet-built fighters and bombers, and a navy supplied by Moscow.

Meanwhile Maphilindo has died. The Philippines has maintained a position in the Indonesia-Malaysia conflict about halfway between the two countries. Though establishing consular ties with Malaysia, it has refused to grant full diplomatic recognition to the Federation. It has kept alive but has not pressed its claim to Sabah. It has continued to maintain friendly relations with Indonesia and to urge on Jakarta a peaceful settlement with Malaysia.

Yet the Philippines also displays a growing uneasiness about Indonesian aims. The infiltration of Indonesians, many of them Communists, into the southern Philippine island of Mindanao and Jakarta's growing collaboration with Peking are beginning to worry the Philippine government. Manila's desire to demonstrate an Asian-minded nationalism through harmony with anti-Western Indonesia has come to seem increasingly loaded with danger.

As for Malaysia, its resoluteness and the strong British Commonwealth support it has received have kept Indonesia as of late 1965 from turning the battle into a major war. Afraid to challenge Commonwealth forces, Jakarta has fallen back on a policy of maintaining pressure on Malaysia through guerrilla infiltrations, the trade embargo and international maneuvering. Indonesia seemed to be waiting for a favorable break such as internal disintegration of the patchwork Malaysian state or a Communist victory in Vietnam. Singapore's withdrawal from Malaysia in August, 1965, did not signify the break-up of Malaysia that Jakarta had hoped for. Singapore continued mutual defense arrangements with Malaysia and left intact Britain's use of Singapore as an air and naval base.

In all, the Indonesian confrontation of Malaysia has created a crisis only a shade less serious than the fighting in Vietnam. Communist China is backing the hostile action with economic aid to Indonesia and worldwide propaganda support; the Soviet Union is assisting Jakarta both militarily and economically. Early in 1965 Indonesia withdrew from the United Nations when Malaysia was named a temporary member of the Security Council. Sukarno has threatened to sponsor a second United Nations, possibly in cooperation with Communist China, consisting of what he calls the "New Emerging Forces"—new nations and old ones with new Socialist and Communist governments—to rival the "Old Established Forces," meaning the Western nations that have exercised world domination.

Cambodia is the focus of still another serious conflict between Southeast Asian countries. The basis is historical and emotional. Prince Sihanouk, Cambodia's chief of state, has never forgotten that

in olden days the Thais and Vietnamese overran the
Cambodians. He believes they plan to do it again.
The fact that Thailand and South Vietnam are allies
of the United States has made the Prince hostile toward the United States. Under these circumstances
he has turned to Communist China.

Cambodia's troubles with Thailand and Vietnam
have taken the form of occasional border clashes
and threatening charges and countercharges. Prince
Sihanouk contends that South Vietnamese and Thai
troops have advanced beyond his border and that
the two countries shelter rebels who scheme to overthrow him. For their part, the South Vietnamese
and Thais maintain that Cambodia protects Communists and supports Vietcong aggression. For
years Cambodia and Thailand quarreled furiously
over an ancient Khmer temple on their border. The
International Court of Justice finally ruled that it
belonged to Cambodia.

Prince Sihanouk's attitude is conditioned by the
fact that he is convinced the Communists and, in
particular, Communist China are going to triumph
in his part of Southeast Asia. He wants to be on the
winning side, although in his candid moments he
emphasizes that he does not like Communism and
that he doubts he would have much of a future if the
Communists took Cambodia.

Prince Sihanouk's anti-American tendencies led
him in 1963 to refuse United States aid, which was

paying for his 30,000-man armed forces among
other things. In May, 1965, he terminated diplomatic relations with the United States. Peking has
encouraged such gestures, but has carefully side-
stepped Prince Sihanouk's pleas for specific guar-
antees that Communist China would fight for
Cambodia's defense. Peking's assurances have been
confined to general statements of full support for
Cambodia in case of aggression against it. Peking
doubtless is reluctant to make any specific guaran-
tees to a country with which Communist China has
no common border. Military intervention by Communist China in Cambodia would be disastrous for
the Chinese Communists if the United States chose
to oppose it.

There is little prospect that Cambodia's quarrels
with its neighbors will cease until the conflict between Communist and anti-Communist forces in
Southeast Asia has been settled one way or the
other.

XII

The Keys to the Future

IN AN ARTICLE in *The New York Times* I once observed that the new countries of Southeast Asia could not reach a high level of social, political and economic development until they had worked themselves out of their confused and emotional state of extreme nationalism. And the process, I said, might take a generation or two.

This, of course, was a comment on only one of Southeast Asia's problems. As earlier chapters have indicated, there are many others. They include overpopulation, inexperience in self-government, general poverty, the low level of education, shortage of capital, the effects of the struggle for and against Communism, and the pressures of powerful outside forces. Nationalism as it shows itself in Southeast

Asia is in some ways a unifying and constructive element. But because it hinders rational analysis and sober tackling of problems and subordinates the material welfare of whole population groups to emotional resentments and hostilities, it is generally a major barrier to progress. It blocks many avenues of cooperation with outside countries, particularly those of the West, that could contribute enormously to social, political and economic advancement.

Nationalism, therefore, must be classed as one of the basic forces now affecting the future of Southeast Asia. It ranks with the Communist drive for power, the counterdrive to defeat Communism, and the related thrusts and maneuvers in the area by Communist China and the Soviet Union on the one hand and the United States and its allies on the other.

In Southeast Asia today it is Indonesia that exhibits the most fervent and aggressive nationalism—a nationalism that may become a new imperialism. Though at present misgoverned, disorganized and economically weak and chaotic, Indonesia is nevertheless the fifth most populous nation of the world and is potentially one of the richest. Even today it must be classed as a power center, a country whose actions deeply affect the destinies of other lands. In fact, it may be that Indonesia has decided to try to turn the southern semicircle of Southeast Asian nations into its sphere of domination.

On a visit to the Philippines in early May, 1965, I was struck by the strength and subversive character of the influence that Indonesia was already exercising there. In the daily *Manila Bulletin* on the morning of my arrival, there appeared this item:

> Ambassador-designate Abdul Karim Rashid of Indonesia—who will tomorrow take over the post being vacated by Ambassador Nazir Pamontjak—was born in Malaya and expelled from Thailand as Indonesia's military attaché for secret dealings with Chinese Communists. A major in the Indonesian Army and former chief of the Indonesian secret service in Jakarta, the incoming Indonesian envoy was declared *persona non grata* by the Thai government in February, 1965.

> Rashid was appointed as Indonesian Ambassador to the Philippines after the government had declined to give an agreement to Jakarta's first nominee, Lieutenant-General Djatikusumo, who while consul-general in Singapore organized an espionage network in preparation for the confrontation policy against Malaysia.

Indonesia has hundreds of agents like Ambassador Rashid in the Philippines. The day before I arrived in Manila an Indonesian named Iljas Bakri, who had been in the Philippines for seven years doing university studies that he carefully never quite managed to finish, left for Jakarta under charges of subversive activity. Philippine authorities had discovered he was a "professional" student, a person who uses his stay at a university year after year as a cover while he secretly serves as a political agent. The authorities had found that Bakri had collected intelligence, led anti-American demonstrations and spread pro-Indonesian and Communist propaganda among Filipino students.

Jakarta's agents emphasize the Malay heritage that Filipinos and Indonesians have in common, call on Filipinos to throw off the "un-Filipino" influence of the United States, foster general discontent over existing social conditions and promote Marxist ideas. Many of the agents are Communists who mix support of Communism with movements for Malay nationalism, Asian nationalism and anti-Western nationalism. A large embassy in Manila and a big consular establishment in Davao, capital of the southern Philippine island of Mindanao, are centers of Indonesian activity. Indonesians disperse money, free trips to Indonesia and other favors to certain Filipino journalists who will recommend the Indonesian "line."

Misdirected nationalism exists in varying degrees in other Southeast Asian countries. A growing anti-American Filipino nationalism among students, intellectuals and young businessmen eases the task of

Indonesian agents and erects barriers to the economic development of the Philippines. Mounting obstacles to American investment in the Philippines and to the operation of American businesses there hinder the flow of American capital to a country that cannot possibly gather enough capital of its own to achieve major economic growth.

Before Western colonization Southeast Asia had close trade and cultural relations with China. Peking's aims are to make the entire area, or at least the northern group of Southeast Asian states, a sphere of Chinese domination. Moving increasingly close to Communist China, Indonesia denounces United States efforts to save South Vietnam from Communist conquest, and Indonesian groups talk of sending "volunteers" to fight for North Vietnam. Thus, Indonesia and Communist China loom in Southeast Asian affairs as an aggressive north-south alliance.

At present Peking is attempting to advance through substitutes. Acting on the belief that United States power and influence are the chief obstacles to its goals, Communist China supports and encourages any force that is hostile to the United States. Thus, non-Communist but anti-American Ne Win of Burma and Sihanouk of Cambodia, as well as pro-Communist and anti-American Sukarno of Indonesia and the North Vietnamese and other Communists, all get Peking's support. Communist China operates on the theory that if the United States can be pushed out of Southeast Asia, the region will become an easy target for Chinese influence and take-over.

Too far removed from Southeast Asia to effectively use direct military pressure, Moscow has promoted its influence in the area through propaganda and economic and military aid. The Soviet Union has the double-barreled objective of undermining both the United States and Communist China. Peking and Moscow compete for the allegiance of the Southeast Asian Communist movements, a rivalry that is most sharply seen in Vietnam. There the Communists desperately need military aid from both the Soviet Union and Communist China, but are pushed and pulled as each power urges Hanoi to have as little to do with the other as possible. For weeks during early 1965 Communist China simply held up the passage through its territory of Soviet military equipment destined for North Vietnam.

United States troops in Vietnam, the British defense treaty with Malaysia, the United States defense agreement with the Philippines, United States military aid and training missions in Thailand and the Philippines, and the Southeast Asia Treaty Organization are the main instruments through which the anti-Communist effort in Southeast Asia is organized.

The members of SEATO are the United States,

Britain, Australia, New Zealand, France, the Philippines, Pakistan and Thailand. Its headquarters are in Bangkok. The alliance is the result mainly of an American effort after the Communist victory over the French in Indochina. The aim of that effort was to unite international forces against any further Communist gains in Southeast Asia. Americans and especially the British hoped to get the southern Asian as well as most of the Southeast Asian countries into an anti-Communist pact, but the late Prime Minister Nehru of India refused to consider joining. Neutralist Burma, Indonesia and Ceylon followed Nehru's lead. The 1954 Geneva agreements barred the Indochinese countries from joining such a pact.

The SEATO treaty was signed in Manila in September, 1954. The signers agreed that, should any of them be attacked, each would "act to meet the common danger in accordance with its constitutional processes." This pledge was specifically extended to cover three non-signers—South Vietnam, Cambodia and Laos—should these countries ask for SEATO aid. The United States added to the treaty a declaration that Washington considered its responsibilities under the pact to apply only to Communist aggression. Thus, the treaty did not involve the United States or any other signer in such disputes as Pakistan's quarrel with India or Cambodia's struggles with Thailand and South Vietnam.

It is easy to belittle the importance and accomplishments of SEATO. Certainly the Organization has had serious defects. Neither Pakistan nor France has ever really felt committed to its basic aim of opposing Communism and Communist China in Southeast Asia; both have had their own private axes to grind. Pakistan joined SEATO in the hope of getting support in its running quarrel with India. It has since become increasingly friendly with Peking and would ignore any SEATO decision to take military action against Communist China. France has worked against the spirit of the treaty ever since it was signed, by trying to promote a South Vietnamese settlement with North Vietnam that many people believe would result in a Communist take-over of the whole country. Another deficiency of SEATO has been that, because of the weakness of its Asian membership, it has had to rely too heavily on United States power.

But, over all, SEATO has been worthwhile. Its annual joint military exercises, the exchange of information and opinion among members, and the common countermeasures against Communist subversion have strengthened the ability of the members to combat Communism. In addition, all SEATO members except France have followed an interpretation of the treaty worked out by the United States and Thailand—that any single member of SEATO can come to the aid of another regardless of whether the whole Organization has decided on an action. This Thai-American interpretation resulted from the failure of treaty members to approve SEATO action in Laos in 1961 when Communist-led Pathet Lao forces threatened to take over the kingdom. Neither France nor Britain favored intervention and they were successful in blocking it.

It is to SEATO's credit that it has aided efforts to defeat Communist aggression in Vietnam. Action by the United States in Vietnam, taken under joint agreements between Washington and Saigon, has had SEATO approval. Australia's obligations under SEATO led to the dispatch of a battalion of Australian troops to fight in Vietnam. The SEATO treaty enabled South Vietnam to call in early May, 1965, for troops from the Philippines. Action on the call was still pending in late 1965. In spite of French abstention and some qualifying amendments by Pakistan, the 1965 annual meeting of SEATO foreign ministers adopted a strong resolution calling for support of the anti-Communist war in Vietnam and of Malaysia's resistance to Indonesian aggression. These developments show that, though SEATO's role is limited, it is important.

In the foreseeable future the shape of things all through Southeast Asia will depend largely on the outcome of the struggle against Communism in Vietnam and Laos. If the Communists are defeated in

South Vietnam, prospects will brighten for all Southeast Asia. Indonesia would very likely ease its drive against Malaysia eventually and possibly drop it. Cambodia, no longer confident of Communist success in Asia, would probably come to some form of live-and-let-live terms with its Thai and Vietnamese neighbors. Democratic forces and tendencies would be strengthened throughout the area. The United States and other countries could be expected to start new aid programs that would increase the chances of dealing successfully with some basic economic and social problems. With less Communist interference and a rise in the prestige of the United States and the West in general, even nationalism might become less irrational and damaging.

Outright anti-Communist victory in Vietnam, of course, seems less likely than a negotiated compromise. But any settlement that clears the Vietcong threat from South Vietnam would be a kind of victory and a considerable Vietcong defeat even if North Vietnam is left under its present government. Constructive results would follow—at least until the Communists felt strong enough to try again.

Vietcong victory, with United States withdrawal from Vietnam, would bring the Communists to power in all Vietnam and Laos. Communist pressure would then be strongly turned on Thailand; if the Thais resisted, another long and bloody struggle would loom. Cambodia, if not taken over directly by the Communists, would become a Communist satellite with little freedom of action.

The simple if unacceptable fact is that Southeast Asia is too weak at the present stage of history to determine its own destiny. It must rely on the United States and its allies to protect it from direct and indirect Chinese Communist domination, or accept that domination and make do with being a Chinese sphere of power and influence. Soviet interests lie in cooperating with the United States in blocking the Chinese—and Peking accuses Moscow of doing just that. But so far, the pull of Communism plus deep hostility to and suspicion of the United States have prevented Moscow from openly harmonizing its policy with Washington's. A real Soviet shift of position could change Southeast Asia's prospects dramatically for the better.

About the only way that Southeast Asia could ever cease to be a battlefield for outside powers and a center of conflict between its own component states would be for the Southeast Asian countries to drop their quarrels with each other and come together in agreements for regional cooperation. In this way the region could be strong enough to face the rest of the world as an independent force.

INDEX

TILLMAN DURDIN

Tillman Durdin, veteran foreign correspondent of *The New York Times*, has been reporting the news from Southeast Asia and other parts of the Far East for more than 25 years.

Born in Pecos, Texas, Mr. Durdin was editor of the Pecos weekly newspaper before he graduated from high school. Later he worked for *The Los Angeles Times* and *The San Antonio Express* before shipping as a seaman in 1930 to see the world. Stopping off at Shanghai, he entered journalism there and eventually became managing editor of the English-language daily *The China Press*.

When the China-Japan war broke out in 1937 Mr. Durdin joined *The New York Times* and spent the next four years covering the Chinese side of the fighting. During World War II he was a war correspondent in Malaya, the Southwest Pacific, Burma and India. At the end of the war he reestablished the *Times* bureau in China as its chief and reported the Communist takeover of the country. After a year as a Nieman Fellow at Harvard, Mr. Durdin was chief of *Times* bureaus covering Southeast Asia, Hong Kong, Taiwan and mainland China. In this capacity he traveled constantly, reporting the wars and political changes throughout this vast area, with periods in Japan, India, North Africa and Europe as well. In 1961 he was called to New York to become Far East specialist on the Editorial Board of *The Times*. In 1964 he was assigned to head a new *Times* bureau for the Southwest Pacific with headquarters in Sydney, Australia.